# Teddy's Child

ALSO BY VIRGINIA VAN DER VEER HAMILTON

BIOGRAPHY

*Hugo Black: The Alabama Years*

*Lister Hill: Statesman from the South*

*Hugo Black and the Bill of Rights* (editor)

AUTOBIOGRAPHY

*Looking for Clark Gable and Other 20th-Century Pursuits: Collected Writings*

*Taking Off the White Gloves: Southern Women and Women Historians* (contributor)

STATE HISTORY

*Alabama: A Bicentennial History*

*Seeing Historic Alabama: Fifteen Guided Tours* (2nd Edition, with Jacqueline A. Matte)

TEXTBOOKS

*Your Alabama*

*The Story of Alabama*

# TEDDY'S CHILD

## Growing Up in the Anxious Southern Gentry Between the Great Wars

~ *A Family Memoir* ~

### VIRGINIA VAN DER VEER HAMILTON

*Virginia Van der Veer Hamilton*

NEWSOUTH BOOKS

Montgomery | Louisville

NewSouth Books
105 South Court Street
Montgomery, AL 36104

Library of Congress Cataloging-in-Publication Data

Hamilton, Virginia Van der Veer.
Teddy's child : growing up in the anxious Southern gentry between the great
wars : a family memoir / Virginia Van der Veer Hamilton.
p. cm.

ISBN-13: 978-1-58838-195-8
ISBN-10: 1-58838-195-1

1. Hamilton, Virginia Van der Veer—Childhood and youth. 2. Birmingham
(Ala.)—Social life and customs—20th century. 3. Depressions—1929—
Alabama—Birmingham. 4. Frankfort (Ky.)—Social life and customs—
20th century. 5. Hamilton, Virginia Van der Veer—Family. I. Title.
F334.B65H36 2009
976.1'781062092—dc22

2009006385
Printed in the United States of America

*For my aunt*

ELIZABETH VAN DER VEER (1901–1993)

*whose diary, short stories, oral history, snapshots, and habit of holding onto*

*family memorabilia were essential to my telling of this story*

# Contents

# PREFACE

I had a lot of help writing this book. Almost all of the members of my immediate family being writers—or would-be writers, they left a long and, at times, revealing paper trail.

Miss Rose, my father's mother, kept a journal until the events she had to record became too painful; then she took up writing letters to people she admired, Herbert Hoover in particular. My father's father, whom I was instructed to call Daddy or Daddy Mac—although silent and withdrawn for long periods—wrote a lengthy letter alluding to our family trait, extreme anxiety; that letter has survived.

My uncle Stewart was a Red Cross ambulance driver in Italy during the first World War; his letters to family members back home were carefully preserved as we moved hither, thither, and yon. Stewart also wrote three bad novels and quite a few short stories published in magazines known as "pulps" for the cheap paper on which they were printed; these bear absolutely no relation to the reality of our lives. But I did draw some material from an unpublished autobiographical novel that my uncle wrote in his old age, making allowances for Stewart's irresistible urge to romanticize.

My aunt Elizabeth, too, wrote for the pulps, specializing in a genre about which she knew virtually nothing: love stories. But Elizabeth kept a diary; I am convinced that the entries in this little, green leather book are as close as I will get to the truth of how things were. I, too, kept a diary in my tenth and eleventh years and again when I was fifteen; these helped me to recollect minutiae of my childhood and adolescence.

My father—the Teddy of this title—wrote thousands of editorials dealing with serious matters of the late 1930s, always stressing the editorial "we" as if these thoughts came from a living entity known as the *Birmingham Age-Herald*. Actually Father alone wrote these high-minded editorials; I recognize them immediately by their preachy tone and their constant themes of love and peace.

Trying to come to grips with his nervous breakdown—the defining experience of his life—Father wrote a novel that was never published; his descriptions of his agony ring harrowingly true. Father's nervous breakdown had been kept a secret from me; I knew only Father the omniscient, the repository of all righteousness and wisdom. So I rely on him to tell this part of our story.

The only member of my family who left no written record was my mother. Dorothy was never one to reveal her inner thoughts; besides, she was too busy sheltering Father and saving him from total despair.

I take these writings to be my rightful inheritance, my family having accumulated little or no money to pass down. In using excerpts from Father's and Stewart's autobiographical novels, I tell myself that I am putting them to their intended use—publication. Miss Rose, loving attention as she did, would have raised no objection to my use of her journal and her letters. Besides, she had torn from her journal the pages she did not want anyone to read. Elizabeth, always meek and agreeable, would not have minded my quoting her diary, there being in it no embarrassing descriptions of sex—indeed, no references to sex whatsoever. I am indebted to Elizabeth also for the rich pictorial legacy of our family, she being the keeper of the scrapbooks and the person who most often aimed the Brownie. The result is a remarkable collection of snapshots and yellowed clippings that testify to the details of the story I am about to relate.

So, Miss Rose, Daddy Mac, Stewart, Elizabeth, and Father—thank you for the use of your writings. And thank you for rearing me during hard times in a family like no other. What fun we had!

# FAMILY SOURCES

*My family members and their works quoted in this memoir:*

McCLELLAN VAN DER VEER (my father):
"Ted," "Teddy," "Father"
> "Though He Falters," an unpublished autobiographical novel. The text is
> available at the University of Alabama at Birmingham Archives.
> One of his thousands of editorials.

DOROTHY RAINOLD VAN DER VEER (my mother):
"Uvvy"

ROSE STEWART VAN DER VEER (my grandmother):
"Miss Rose," "Mummy," "Mama"
> Journal kept when she lived in Kentucky, now housed in the Kentucky
> Historical Society, Frankfort, Kentucky.
> Excerpts from one of her letters to ex-President Herbert Hoover; Herbert
> Hoover Presidential Library, West Branch, Iowa.

JOHN McCLELLAND* VAN DER VEER* (my grandfather):
"Mac," "Daddy"
> Letter to his son Stewart.
> *His surname was originally spelled Van Derveer. Miss Rose changed it to
> Van der Veer to conform to a family crest she ordered from Holland.
> His son, also named McClelland, dropped the "d."

STEWART VAN DER VEER (my uncle):
"Stewart," "Uncle"

Letters to his parents from the Italian front, 1919, and "Walk in My Moccasins," an unpublished autobiographical novel; both housed in the Birmingham Public Library Archives.

Excerpt from one of his Western stories written for the pulp magazines of the 1930s.

Article on possum hunting in the magazine *Field and Stream* (adapted and personalized by the author).

ELIZABETH VAN DER VEER (my aunt)

Personal diary.

Excerpt from a short story in the pulp magazine *Thrilling Love.*

"Almost Like a Storybook: A Childhood in the Capital of Kentucky, 1901–10," Elizabeth Van der Veer's oral history edited by Virginia Van der Veer Hamilton, *The Register* of the Kentucky Historical Society, Vol. 103, No. 3, Summer 2005.

VIRGINIA VAN DER VEER HAMILTON (author)

Diaries; from ages ten, eleven, and fifteen.

The "Papers of Virginia Van der Veer Hamilton," including my writings over a period of more than fifty years, as well as personal data, general research files, and recorded interviews, manuscripts, correspondence related to research and publishing, and numerous photos and newspaper clippings have been indexed and are open for research in the Department of Archives and Manuscripts, Birmingham Public Library.

## AUTHOR'S NOTE

In the spirit of disclosure, I inform readers that Rose and Mac Van der Veer had another daughter a couple of years older than Elizabeth. This daughter married and, during the years covered in this memoir, 1924–37, she did not live in our neighborhood and had no influence on my upbringing. She suffered most of her life from ill health; she died in 1964. Out of respect for her privacy and that of her descendants, I have omitted her from this family account.

Names of a few others who appear in this memoir have also been changed to protect their privacy.

# Teddy's Child

*With Father and "Uvvy" during hard times.*

# The Arrival

In years to come, Lee Ola—my aunt Elizabeth's friend—almost never passes up a chance to tell about our arrival in Birmingham:

*Why, Virginia, I can see it as clearly as if it were yesterday, you gettin' off the train from New York City, holdin' your mother's hand. I can still see Dorothy, so young and pretty. And Teddy, so tall and good lookin'. You were the most precious little girl, all those golden curls. That was 1925. You must have been about four years old.*

Like other Southern ladies, Lee Ola keeps a vast fund of dates at her command, birth dates in particular. But I have my doubts about those curls. Unless my mother, the night before, had wound my fine, straight hair into tight balls tied with little white rags.

In her telling, Lee Ola leaves out one essential fact. Probably she is unaware of the reason that my parents have left New York. Elizabeth would have glossed over it:

*How 'bout carryin' me to the Terminal Station in your big automobile, Lee Ola, to pick up Teddy, Dorothy, and Virginia? They're going to stay with us awhile. Teddy's been working too hard at that newspaper. He needs a good rest.*

Lee Ola would have seen at first glance that Teddy Van der Veer, at twenty-nine, is one of the handsomest men she has ever laid eyes on. Without a doubt, at six feet three, one of the tallest. Broad-shouldered. Profile like John Gilbert or John Barrymore. Too bad, Lee Ola probably thinks, that poor Elizabeth didn't get her share of those good looks.

But Lee Ola is so busy welcoming us, in her flirty way, that she fails to notice little signals of distress. Teddy's big hands tremble as he points out our luggage to the porter. His voice quavers. His breath comes in little shallow gasps as if he has run to Birmingham.

Although Elizabeth and Lee Ola have no way of knowing this, Teddy's heart is beating erratically, his long legs feel shaky and numb, his palms are sweating. My young father is overwhelmed by the Great Fear. He imagines all manner of catastrophes. Worst of all, he imagines that he is dying.

> TED: I can't get away from the feeling that I might die . . . you crazy fool, you're no nearer dying than . . . there's nothing the matter with your heart . . . except that you yourself have got it in a state of perpetual excitement.

A New York City doctor has assured Ted that nothing is wrong with his heart. But this patient is functioning only about 40 percent of normal: the problem lies elsewhere.

The doctor tells Ted that he is suffering from neurasthenia. Commonly known back then as nervous exhaustion, nervous prostration, or nervous breakdown.

Leave New York, the doctor prescribes. Go to a warmer climate. Give up all mental work for several months. Chop wood, hoe weeds, rest. That's the sum total of his advice. But he cautions his patient: This process is going to take all the courage you've got. And it's going to take time.

Time? My father and mother have only five hundred dollars to their names. At best, this would last only three months in New York. That's the real reason we have come to Birmingham. *To take shelter with the family.*

BY MIDDAY IN FEBRUARY, Birmingham would have been smothered, as usual, beneath a dark cloud of oily smoke, quick to leave its imprint on white shirts and lace curtains. This smoke drifts down like fog, forcing motorists like Lee Ola to switch on their headlights at midday and creep along lest they smack into pedestrians or other automobiles.

My mother, reared in lush New Orleans, educated on the picture-postcard campus of Wellesley College, must have been shocked at her first sight of this gritty town. Don't fuss about smoke, Birmingham citizens retort. Smoke means that steel mills, pig iron factories, coal mines, and smelters are busy. Smoke means pay checks. Smoke means good times.

As Lee Ola inches her Dodge away from Terminal Station, Dorothy cannot miss seeing a huge sign, outlined in white lightbulbs:

*Birmingham, the Magic City.*

WHAT AN ARTFUL SLOGAN! Under its spell, men by the hundreds packed up wives and children, abandoned hardscrabble farms or backwater towns, and set out to claim a share of that magic. In faraway Kansas City, Missouri, my grandfather, Mac Van der Veer, also fell for this artifice. He must not have heard Birmingham's less flattering nicknames:

*Bad Birmingham*

*Murder Capital of the World*

Mac had no idea that he was moving his family to the home of the biggest Ku Klux Klan klavern in Alabama, named for Robert E. Lee. That the overwhelming majority of their fellow citizens would be blue collar folk fresh off the farm—or the boat. That children by the hundreds worked dawn to dusk in cotton mills and coal mines.

*Where we arrived—the Terminal Station—and what we saw. Courtesy of Birmingham Public Library Archives.*

But my grandfather could scarcely have been unaware that Birmingham in the early 1920s was known to be a hotbed of anti-Catholicism. He must have read in the *Kansas City Star* about the fatal shooting of a Catholic priest by an itinerant Methodist preacher in broad daylight in downtown Birmingham. Jurors in that sensational case, beguiled by a clever defense attorney, Hugo Lafayette Black, found the assailant not guilty.

Those matters aside, Mac figured that his elder son, Stewart, with his knack for words, could make a good living by starting his own advertising business in a new and growing city. Perhaps his daughter, Elizabeth, when back in her native South, would find herself a husband before she became an old maid. Most of all, Mac hoped that his wife, Rose, would be pleased with Birmingham's climate. Cooler in summer than sweltering New Orleans. Warmer in winter than other places they have lived in the tumultuous course of their marriage: Frankfort, Kentucky; Enid, Oklahoma; and Kansas City, Missouri.

LEE OLA TRANSPORTS us and our luggage in an easterly direction. We head away from the smoke and soot of the steel mills. But we definitely do not head toward a fashionable residential area south of downtown Birmingham, known locally as Over the Mountain.

My grandmother—almost everyone calls her Miss Rose—has this thing about mountains. In later years, when we drive across the plains of Texas or Kansas on family vacations, Miss Rose, in her big white hat, veil, and gloves, keeps hopping out of the car and rushing up to filling station attendants demanding to know—although the earth's surface is perfectly flat in all directions, clear to the horizon:

Are there any *mountains* up ahead?

This particular phobia is easily dealt with: just stay on level ground. Miss Rose has no intention of living on the slopes of Red Mountain, much less *over* the mountain. Not that Red Mountain is all that steep; at its highest point, it looms above Jones Valley barely 1,000 feet. But to placate Miss Rose, my family settles more than sixty-five blocks east of Terminal Station, nothing separating us from downtown higher than the gentle slopes of the First Avenue viaduct, which raises automobiles, yellow streetcars, and occasional pedestrians safely past Sloss Furnace. If we drive across the viaduct as Sloss Furnace disgorges a stream of molten pig iron fiery enough to light up the night sky for miles around,

Miss Rose is unperturbed. She is afraid of mountains, not fire.

A sub-reason that my family chose to live in Roebuck Springs is so that Stewart could keep horses—as we always expressed it—*on the place.* No one stopped to consider that Elizabeth would be unlikely to make a suitable match in this remote and déclassé part of town.

THUS, ON THE day of our arrival, Lee Ola and Elizabeth deliver my mother, my father, and me to a setting selected by Mac, Miss Rose, and Stewart because of two themes that resonate throughout our lives like clashing cymbals:

*The Great Fear* (in this case, Miss Rose's problem with mountains) accompanied by *High Romanticism* (in this instance, Mac succumbing to the lure of a Magic City and Stewart fancying himself a cowboy).

*Getting acquainted with Stewart's hounds and Inky.*

We leave paved First Avenue and bump along muddy roads. I peer through the murky isinglass that covers the sides of Lee Ola's big Dodge. This neighborhood contains a few houses, widely separated, and, like my former playground, New York's Central Park, a lot of trees.

As we pull up a long chirt driveway, Lee Ola sounds her horn:

*Good-oo-ga!*

*Good-oo-ga!*

Four hounds in the front yard begin to bay, each in a different key. A woman on the porch, dressed entirely in white (in February!), claps her hands with joy. When Lee Ola cuts the engine, my grandmother calls out what I will come to expect as her invariable greeting: Thank goodness you're here! I was *afraid* something had happened . . .

FOR MY FATHER, the first night in Birmingham was not an easy one.

TED: All [he] needed was a few weeks of rest. But suppose that wild fear that he had known in New York should seize him again and, hour after hour, sweep over him in endless, ever higher, black waves?

God, how quiet it was! Not a sound. Then a dog's sharp bark. Involuntarily he started.

*"All right, Ted?" Dorothy asked.*

*"Yes, only a little restless. Strange bed."*

Suppose he shouldn't be able to shake off his fears at all? The doctor had admitted that it would be a hard fight. Suppose he didn't have it in him to win? Here was that damn perspiration bursting out all over him again. The covers were stifling him. He pushed the spread and comforter off his shoulders. No, that wouldn't do. He felt damp. It might give him a cold.

There was that dog again! Tensely he waited for the barking to stop. It might keep up for hours. He wouldn't be able to stand that. Ah, thank God, the dog seemed to be stopping. There were longer intervals between his yelps. No! God damn the brute, he was hard at it again.

Should he get up? No! Not if he died lying here. Nothing could happen if he lay still except for him to die. He would die if necessary. He would not get up! He would simply have to submit to whatever agonies might come. Let the cold sweat, the dread thought, the tingling nerves and muscles combine against him how they would! He would not cry out!

There was one thing that made him feel easier. If he would, all at once, go to pieces—he might simply start shaking or crying or shrieking and be unable to stop—well, he would not be on Dorothy's hands alone. That wouldn't be so terrible as it would have been if something like this had happened in New York.

PART ONE

*How It All Began*

# To the Reader

*When I read a work of nonfiction in which the author digresses from the main narrative to recount family history, I find myself skimming across those pages or skipping them altogether. Yet here I am, offering a similar look back on the major figures in this memoir. If you choose not to read How It All Began and Out of Place, you will miss, among other vignettes:*

*Miss Rose's glory days as a belle, Teddy's lost opportunity to pitch in a World Series baseball game, and Stewart's encounter on the Italian front in the first World War with fellow ambulance driver Ernest Hemingway.*

*If you skip this section, you will not be as able to comprehend the contrast between our family's bright prospects in the Bluegrass region of Kentucky during the* fin de siècle *and the stark situation in which we found ourselves in industrial Birmingham, Alabama, during the Great Depression.*

*Above all, you will miss the early warning signs of the high anxiety that afflicted our family.*

# The Belle of the Bluegrass

Miss Rose prevails upon a neighbor to give her a ride to the end of the car line. Streetcar line, that is. Also known as the Loop because two streetcars, number twenty-five and number thirty-eight, turn around here and head back to downtown Birmingham.

As one of the first passengers, she gets a window seat and, eventually, a seatmate. White for sure, black riders being relegated to the rear. Perhaps a housewife bound for Woolworth's to buy six spools of thread. Or a salesgirl in the ladies' lingerie department at Loveman, Joseph & Loeb. Or a teller at Birmingham Trust Bank. Miss Rose herself is headed for Pizitz Department Store to purchase a pair of white gloves.

On a good day—one on which the streetcar does not have to double as a snow plow—it takes thirty minutes to arrive at First Avenue and Nineteenth Street, what with stopping to pick up new passengers almost every block.

Fixing her blue eyes on her seatmate, Miss Rose opens with the only topic that she and this chance acquaintance have in common:

*Where I grew up, we never had this much rain in the winter.*

Pause. A polite nod from the bank teller.

*I was the Belle of the Bluegrass, you know!*

The housewife, the salesgirl, or the teller shifts ever so slightly toward the aisle. This old lady must be a nut. Who ever heard of wearing *white* clothes in the middle of winter? Who ever heard of *blue* grass?

Miss Rose is undeterred. Like some Ancient Mariner, she repeats this remark to all and sundry, puzzling many a grocery boy, postman, cook, neighbor, and anyone who chances to share her pew at the Independent Presbyterian Church.

Her boast being true—she has a slew of newspaper clippings to prove it—

11

what is this once-famous belle doing in Birmingham, Alabama, of all improbable places? Riding streetcar number twenty-five with people who never even *heard* of the Bluegrass?

Oh Rose, how did it come to this?

Her grown children have long since had their fill of Miss Rose's tales of her glory days. Mac, too, would prefer to let this subject drop. Thus my arrival strikes my grandmother as heaven-sent. In a few years, this child will be old enough to sit quietly and listen, if bribed by a plate of tea cakes and a glass of lemonade. Then Miss Rose will show me an old, red ledger in which she had pasted a jumble of mementos, including a number of faded clippings from the *Lexington Herald*, *Frankfort Capital*, and *Louisville Courier-Journal*.

Now pay attention, Virginia, this is what it says about me in the newspaper:

> Rose Stewart has achieved a clean 'walk over' to her position as a belle . . . she numbers victims at her chariot wheels by the score and the fame of her young beauty is widespread. Kentucky boasts no fairer maid.

Miss Rose reads about attending the Pan American Congress at Lexington, along with other Bluegrass beauties, to impress the delegates with Kentucky's trinity: *fine horses, fine whiskey, fine women.*

She reads about a grand ball in Frankfort in 1891 celebrating the fact that this small city has been declared the state's permanent capital. And about the Light Infantry Ball at Lexington honoring Kentucky's new governor, John Young Brown.

*Look, Virginia, here's a drawing of me in the* Lexington Herald. *And this is what is says underneath:*

> The quaint Empire gowns Rose Stewart much effects—her Greek profile in strong relief and her violet eyes upturned.

There was also the big civic festival of 1891 in Cincinnati when the 400-man drill corps of Kentucky Military Institute displayed its flashing bayonets, bright uniforms, and skill at precision marching.

*And see here, Virginia, who they chose as their sponsor!*

The "noted Belles of the Bluegrass" in Rose's party on that banner day included her friends Bertie and Evelyn Brown, daughters of the governor; Henrietta Blackburn, niece of U.S. Senator Joseph Blackburn; and Lucy Hill, daughter of one famous Confederate general, A. P. Hill, and niece of another, John Hunt Morgan.

Hearing these stories so often, I come to regard the Brown girls, "Hen'retta" Blackburn, and other young ladies of Frankfort society as my friends too. I recognize the names of many of the swains who escort Rose. Like M. C. Alford (who is to become Kentucky's lieutenant governor), William F. Grayot (a future Kentucky secretary of state and treasurer of Churchill Downs), and Caswell Bennett (son of the chief justice of the Kentucky Court of Appeals). I learn to roll the storied syllables of Kentucky—John J. Crittenden, John C. Breckinridge, Simon Bolivar Buckner—trippingly on my tongue.

In 1924 when she visited us in New York City, Miss Rose talked herself inside the Democratic National Convention. After hearing her stories, I can easily imagine her telling that doorman:

*I'm a friend of W. C. P. Breckinridge . . . Governor John Young Brown . . . Senator Joseph C. S. Blackburn . . .*

*OK, lady, OK! Go right in!*

Miss Rose shows me, in her old red journal, a photograph of a famous star of Broadway and Hollywood, Pauline Frederick. Beneath this—there being no doubt in her mind as to who is the number one beauty—she has written:

> Pauline Frederick. Said to be *my* double!
> (Why Pauline, you look just like Rose Stewart!)

As the climax of what she calls our little talks, Miss Rose instructs me:

*When you get to Louisville, be sure to go to the Pendennis Club. Tell them who you are* (as always, she avoids the forbidden word granddaughter) *and they'll let you right in!*

ROLLING HER BLUE eyes and, with her index finger, drawing an imaginary circle in the air beside her ear, Miss Rose pronounces loudly:

*Fee-de-da-monk!*

She does not use this expression to refer to the mentally handicapped. She flings it at normal people whom she considers foolish, misguided, or temporarily stupid. Me, on occasion. As a little girl, I take this to be just another of her peculiar expressions—like what she always says at Thanksgiving when Audrey passes the silver casserole filled with oyster dressing:

*Varmints! I don't eat varmints!*

Later I realize that the expression *fee-de-da-monk* must have come straight out of Rose's childhood. She was nine years old when her father, Dr. John Quincy Adams Stewart, embarked upon his sixteen years as superintendent of the Kentucky Institute for the Education and Training of Feeble-Minded Children. Rose lived at what she called the *Ins-stute*, on a high bluff adjoining the Frankfort Cemetery and overlooking Kentucky's capital, until she married at twenty-four.

In those days, most people, even in the medical profession, used harsh terms like idiots, imbeciles, and morons to describe the retarded. Backward was a gentler way of putting it; *fee-de-da-monk* must have been common slang. Most of those unfortunates were boarded in private homes, at fifty to seventy-five dollars apiece for an entire year, without education or training of any kind. Dr. Stewart, in his presidential address to the Kentucky State Medical Association in 1894, declared:

*My very nature is revolted at the idea of farming out those helpless creatures to unkind and mercenary guardians.*

Dr. Stewart presided over the Feeble-Minded Institute like a benevolent despot, regarding his charges of all ages as his children. His was one of the first public institutions in the nation where useful trades were taught. By the standards of the 1890s, my great-grandfather's approach was path-breaking. Boys were taught to make shoes, brooms, and mattresses; girls learned to sew, cook, wash, and perform other household duties. Everyone took part in calisthenics, recitations, and group singing. More advanced students played in a band. As part of her father's training program, Rose had a female patient assigned to serve her sort of like a personal maid.

Being surrounded by the mentally retarded seemed to Rose the most natural thing in the world. Staff and residents alike petted, waited upon, and made much of their superintendent's youngest and prettiest daughter. No wonder Rose grew up expecting always to be the center of attention. When she blossomed into a beautiful young woman, those who lived or worked in this small domain began to address her a bit more formally as *Miss Rose*.

# The Handsome Distillery Manager

With Miss Rose always occupying center stage, people rarely paid attention to her husband. It was not always thus.

Mac Van Derveer (as he spelled it before Rose got hold of a Van der Veer crest) was often spoken of in the 1890s as the handsomest man in Frankfort. Especially when he stood in the choir loft of the First Presbyterian Church and lifted his beautiful voice in "How Great Thou Art," "Just a Closer Walk with Thee," or—his brown eyes, set off by heavy brows, fixed directly on Rose Stewart—"O Love That Wilt Not Let Me Go."

ROSE: Mac is so handsome.

Then, perhaps with some premonition of what is to come, she added:

ROSE: But I wish I didn't love him.

My grandfather does not regale me with tales of his youth. It is left to me to piece his story together, bit by bit over the years, from stories told by my father, uncle, and aunt.

The Civil War drastically changed the course of Mac's life. And, consequently, the lives of his descendants, me included. Simply put, it moved him south of the Ohio River and reduced his circumstances from middle class to penury. His father, Lieutenant John Van Derveer, volunteered for three years' service with the 35th Ohio Regiment, commanded by his older half-brother, Colonel Ferdinand Van Derveer. John slept in open fields. Waded across icy creeks. Crossed the Tennessee River on a raft. Saw men die by the thousands.

Apparently John, unmarried, both parents dead, wrote no letters from the battlefront. But Ferdinand and his son, Harry, in letters home, made passing references to John: he was ill, he was better. He barely escaped capture. On one occasion, he challenged Colonel Edward McCook to a two-man horse race, the prize, $100. He must have been a daring young man.

John made it home to Hamilton, Ohio, married the gifted singer Anna McClelland, and fathered four children. Right from the start, people noticed John's and Anna's oldest child. An elderly resident of Hamilton remembered half a century later:

*I recall the Van der Veer family and the three fine-looking McClelland women in it. We were invited to dinner when "Mac" Van der Veer was a small boy. When the dinner was announced he ran ahead and, standing on a chair, took off the cover of one of the dishes, exclaiming 'Ha! Company things!' Mac was a very handsome boy, so I presume he is a fine looking man.*

Had the war not taken place, Mac might have studied at the Cincinnati Conservatory of Music and become a noted baritone, particularly renowned for his rendition of his favorite aria, "Valentin's Lament" in Gounod's *Faust*: "Even Bravest Heart May Swell in the Moment of Farewell."

More likely, Mac would have become a doctor or, like his famous uncle, Ferdinand, and his dashing father, a lawyer. But John Van Derveer became too ill to practice law. His nerves and health wrecked, he died at thirty-eight. The official cause was given as *dropsy* (an old term for congestive heart failure). Although not killed on the field of battle, John was nonetheless a victim of the war. His death occurred fifteen years before Congress provided pensions for disabled Union veterans and their widows and minor children. Anna Van Derveer was left to support her children as best she could until Mac could take on this responsibility.

In desperation, she moved to Frankfort to live with her sisters, Kate McClelland Mauer and Mary McClelland. (*Taking shelter with the family.*) To help his mother provide for his younger brothers, Dick and Ferdinand, and his sister, Minnie, Mac, at twelve, drove a wagon to deliver groceries to the back doors of the Frankfort gentry.

At fifteen, he got a better job. All day he sat on a high stool and, in his beautiful handwriting, kept the books on barrels of bourbon whiskey produced by Labrot (rhymes with *grow*) & Graham, a small, family-owned distillery on Glenn's Creek near Versailles (Miss Rose teaches me to pronounce this in the Kentucky way:

*Ver-sails*). Eventually Mac was promoted to cashier and manager.

I learn none of this from my grandfather. It must have been too painful for him to recall his bewilderment when he learned, at age twelve, that his father had died. How humiliated he must have felt knocking on back doors to deliver groceries. Most painful of all, how desperately he has tried to live up to the expectations attached to the suitor who—besting many a blueblood—won the hand of Rose Stewart.

*Mac Van Derveer (seated third from left in tie and bowler hat) between Leopold Labrot (on barrel) and James Graham, with the entire workforce of Labrot & Graham, ca. 1885.*

# *Marrying for Love and Beauty*

## (Example 1)

A Kentucky belle was fated to marry. This matter loomed uppermost in Rose's mind in March 1891, the month of her twenty-fourth birthday (a carefully guarded secret). Obviously Rose could have had her pick of numerous men of substance, a bank president, for example, or a railroad attorney, or one who owned his own business. Or, as had her two elder sisters, she might have married a doctor.

But Rose, ever an imp of the perverse, set her heart on a strikingly handsome man with deep brown eyes and a beautiful baritone voice.

> ROSE: Last night Mac came and we had quite a serious talk. It seems there is always something up and I would not be surprised if our affair would wind up shortly. We certainly can't get along this way. He is getting rather tyrannical I think, and he thinks the way I go [out to parties] is too much for any man to stand.

SOUTHERNERS OF PRIVILEGED rearing—even now—discourage their descendants from marrying merely for love and beauty. Parents take a keen interest in assuring that their offspring marry, so to speak, within the ribbons. If, in so doing, two fortunes are united—oil and life insurance, for example, or two Bluegrass horse farms—the matchmakers consider their efforts well expended, the future of their grandchildren assured.

The young woman has prominent teeth? This problem can be fixed. The young man has bandy legs? Who's to know? He is short? Wear your flat shoes.

Yet occasionally a stubborn and willful young woman—a romantic by nature—kicks over the traces, insisting upon taking a mate of impecunious circumstances and little-known ancestry. Unless she is wealthy in her own name, this is usually a mistake, at least from a monetary standpoint. Furthermore—as proved to be the case in my family—such an errant choice is likely to redound for generations to come.

Rose Stewart was one such romantic.

UNDER THE DEPENDENT Pension Act passed by Congress in March 1891, Anna Van Derveer received her husband's back pay of $4,200 and became entitled to a Union pension of seventeen dollars a month. To accept a government pension in those days was considered a form of disgrace; Mac felt this keenly, especially when news of this settlement appeared in the *Frankfort Journal*, Anna being the only Union widow in town. But the pension considerably eased his financial obligations to his mother and sister; finally he felt free to ask Rose's hand in marriage.

Hoping to escape the summer heat, Rose and her family moved for a few weeks to a rustic camp near Frankfort on the banks of Elkhorn Creek.

> ROSE: I remember nothing except glorious moonlit nights and my sweetheart. The month went by like a dream and I only remember that I was perfectly and thoroughly happy . . .

Perfectly and thoroughly happy? Cherish that moment, Rose.

ON JANUARY 20, 1892, during the height of a snowstorm, Rose Stewart married John McClelland Van Derveer in Frankfort's First Presbyterian Church, within whose congregation Union sympathies had run high during the Civil War. The horse-drawn carriage bearing the bride and her father careened precariously down the icy slopes of Town Hill on its way to the 7 P.M. ceremony.

Despite the weather, the church was filled. Governor Brown occupied a front pew, his eldest daughter, Birdie, serving as one of the bride's six attendants. Several of Rose's former beaux, including Lieutenant Governor M. C. Alford and W. F. Grayot, served as groomsmen and ushers. Prominent distillers, as well as a number of members of the Kentucky legislature, braved the storm. Obviously this was an event of the first magnitude in Kentucky's intimate capital.

The ceremony, conducted beneath a canopy of evergreens ornamented with

*Above, Rose Stewart in her wedding dress, 1892. Opposite page, John McClelland "Mac" Van Derveer on the day of his wedding.*

pink roses, was judged a brilliant affair. The *Frankfort Journal* enthused: "The prettiest wedding that has ever taken place in the city."

Birdie Brown and Rose's other attendants wore white gowns, their faces covered with long veils. The bride, carrying a bouquet of pink roses, her gown fashioned along Empire lines, was pronounced, as so often before: "The prettiest lady in all of the Bluegrass region."

Mac, too, had his share of encomiums: "One of the handsomest men in the state. A splendid specimen of physical manhood."

After the ceremony, a group of intrepid guests braved the slick hill to toast the newlyweds at a reception at the home of Rose's parents on the grounds of the Feeble-Minded Institute. Understandably nervous about the hazards of their trip back to town, most guests departed at a relatively early hour. Whereupon the bridal couple went upstairs to Rose's childhood bedroom to begin their long married life.

SEVERAL GUESTS FROM out of town, stranded by the storm, spent that night at the Stewarts' home. Among them was one of Rose's former suitors, John McDowell, a man in his thirties, substantial and well set up in business in Louisville. Obviously a game loser, he had served as an usher at her wedding.

Early the following morning, the telephone rang. Someone asked to speak to John McDowell. This message was taken by the only person up and about so early on the morning following a wedding and a reception: Lily, a resident of the Feeble-Minded Institute who had served as Rose's maid for several years.

Filled with the importance of her task, Lily tapped on the door of Rose's bedroom.

*Who is it?*

*It's Lily, Miss Rose.*

Innocent Lily is about to immortalize herself in our storehouse of family legends, on the verge of becoming the main character in a story told and retold, year in and year out, around the table after Thanksgiving dinner or to break the tedium of a Sunday afternoon on the porch.

*What on earth do you want, Lily? (irritated)*

No matter how many times we hear this story, our family always finds Lily's next words hilarious:

*Is John McDowell in there?*

Roars of laughter from the men, giggles from the women. Faint rise in the color of my grandmother's cheeks (not on account of rouge). My grandfather busily lighting his cigar to mask his amusement.

That's about as prurient as we ever get: picturing in our minds' eyes Rose and Mac in bed behind that door.

# Frankfort

In her glowing account of the wedding of Rose and Mac, the society writer for the *Frankfort Journal* could not resist sharing with her readers the following tidbit:

> The young couple will make their home with the groom's mother on Shelby Street, where their apartments have been handsomely furnished for them by the bride's parents.

So, Frankfort learned—if it did not know this already—that the newlyweds could not afford to buy a house. Or even furnish one. Anna Van Derveer had invested her Union pension in a house; thus she was able to provide her son and his bride with a roof over their heads. *(Taking shelter with the family.)*

After the births of sons Stewart and McClellan (called Teddy), Mac built a house on Shelby Street with a large porch, five bedrooms, and one bathroom. In such a setting, the Van Derveers seemed like a typical, middle-class American family in the waning years of the Victorian era. Except, of course, for their beauty. When Mac and Rose made their entrance at an inaugural ball at the Capital Hotel, Mac in full dress, Rose in a new white gown with lacy top and pinched waist, Frankfort's elite—with a touch of envy—whispered:

*What a handsome couple!*

On Saturday evenings, the family gathered in the parlor for informal musicales, Rose accompanying the singers on the piano. Anna McClelland Van Derveer might be cajoled to sing "'Tis the Last Rose of Summer" as she had sung her favorite aria many years before in the presence of the great Adelina Patti. Mac, as always, sang "Valentin's Lament." Stewart and Teddy, voices cracking on the high notes,

*Opposite page, left, Rose with Teddy, her favorite child. Right, Mac with Teddy (in cap) and Stewart.*

22

offered plaintive tunes: "Danny Boy." "Delia." "I'll Take you Home, Kathleen."

Mac was often asked to sing at funerals. Because he refused to accept pay, grateful family members brought presents to his children at Christmas. As this festive season approached, the quartet from the First Presbyterian Church practiced at the home of their leading soloist. With Mac Van Derveer of Labrot & Graham and George Berry of Old Crow Distillery as lead singers in his choir, the minister of First Presbyterian entertained no notions of preaching against alcohol.

At Easter, Mac and his brother Dick were called upon as soloists at their respective churches. Elizabeth, as a little girl, positioned herself between those churches—only one block apart—where she could hear her father's baritone booming from the First Presbyterian Church and her uncle's tenor, as if a lighter echo, from the Episcopal Church of the Ascension.

William Jennings Bryan spoke at one end of the old arched bridge across the Kentucky River. John Fox, author of *The Little Shepherd of Kingdom Come*; Robert Burns Wilson, famous for a poem entitled "Remember the Maine"; and Paul Sawyier, who would win a measure of fame as a nineteenth-century impressionist, all visited in Rose and Mac's parlor.

As a special treat, Dr. John Stewart, Rose's younger brother, took his sister's children in his Packard to Louisville where they stayed at the Seelbach Hotel and dined at the Pendennis Club, its walls hung with pictures of past winners of the Kentucky Derby.

ROSE'S EGGNOG
1 dozen eggs
1 cup whiskey (or more)
1 pint heavy whipping
cream
10 pounds of sugar
    Beat yellows a long,
long time. Add half of the
sugar slowly while beating.
    Add liquor to yellows
and beat. Beat whites and
add four to 10 teaspoons
of sugar slowly.
    Mix with yellows Add
cream. Whip or not as
desired.
    Can be made early and
put in icebox. Beat before
serving.

Anna McClelland and her sister, Mary, lived only a block away. But their other McClelland aunt, Kate Mauer, seemed a distant and more glamorous figure, having moved to the nation's capital. In an era when a mere handful of women held jobs with the United States government, Kate obtained a position in the Treasury Department, doubtless due to the influence of her first cousin, Julia Dent Grant, widow of former President Ulysses S. Grant.

Needless to say, the Van Derveers did not boast about this kinship in a town that increasingly doted upon the Confederate aspect of its past.

ELIZABETH, AS A child, could reel off the names of bourbons as readily as a modern child can name soft drinks: Green River, Old Crow, Old Granddad, Early Times, Ancient Age, Old Forester, James E. Pepper, and, of course, the brand distilled at Labrot & Graham, Old Oscar Pepper.

Every Saturday, the general manager of Labrot & Graham visited the distillery, about a two-hour drive by horse and buggy out Glenn's Creek Road. Elizabeth liked to make this trip with her father, a buffalo robe over their laps on snowy days, Lizzie, their one-eyed brown mare finding her way without direction from Mac. On this drive, Mac and Elizabeth passed the much larger layout of Old Taylor Distillery owned by Colonel E. H. Taylor, whose brand was famous and whose granddaughter, Frances, was Elizabeth's best friend.

Had they traveled blindfolded, Elizabeth, her father, and Lizzie would have known that they were nearing Labrot & Graham by the pungent aroma of corn cooking in huge pots of limestone water. Country women, seated at wooden, slanted desks, attached celluloid caps to the flat-sided, brown whiskey bottles, pasted labels on the top, front, and back, then wiped those labels dry. When she was judged old enough, Elizabeth, as a special treat, was permitted to help with this task. Mac took special pride in the fact that his employees were seldom, if ever, drunk on the job.

In Kentucky, no stigma attaches to whiskey manufacture. This being big business, prominent distillers rate among the social elite. However Mac, not a native and having embarked on distilling out of necessity, felt slightly ashamed of his means of livelihood. Personally he was an abstainer, bourbon being consumed on Shelby Street only as flavoring for Rose's rich Christmas eggnog.

ROSE, HAVING HAD enough of childbearing, gave herself an abortion a year or two after Elizabeth's birth in 1901. She would keep this a secret, perhaps even from Mac, for half a century; in her old age, she unburdened herself to Elizabeth. Neither had the nerve to speak of details.

In 1905 Rose became pregnant again. Eleanor, named for Rose's sister who had died during childbirth (an ill omen), was born the following year.

Believing her family complete, Rose sought other interests. In June 1908, she sang the role of Pitti-Sing in Gilbert and Sullivan's opera *The Mikado* before a sell-out crowd at the Capital Theater, particularly relishing her solo, "For He's to Marry Yum-Yum."

That fall Baby Eleanor died of pneumonia. Ninety years later, Elizabeth— who had been seven at the time—remembered being taken into the parlor to say good-bye to her sister in a little white coffin by the front window.

Rose took Eleanor's death very hard. For months, she never left her house except—her face hidden by a long veil—to take long walks in alleys and back streets. She blamed herself for Eleanor's death, believing this to have been God's punishment for her abortion of the earlier pregnancy.

She took up New Thought, a philosophy popularized by Ella Wheeler Wilcox, the Dear Abby of her day. Proponents of New Thought believed that, by thinking constructively, humans could mold their bodies and their lives, thus attaining health, prosperity, and other good results. But to Rose, the power of the mind was not the main attraction of New Thought; she desperately wanted to believe—as did many in this movement—in such occult and mystic possibilities as extrasensory perception and reincarnation.

Browsing in Ella Wheeler Wilcox's books on Rose's parlor table, Stewart, at fourteen, came upon New Thought.

> STEWART: Freely admitting—privately, of course—that I was afraid of nearly everything, I read many of my mother's inspirational books, all of which said about the same thing . . . face your fears . . . The mere crossing of a crowded street demands a certain amount of anxiety. However, if

while dodging buggies, carriages, wagons and the occasional automobile, you are plagued by the absurd anticipation of being attacked by Indians, your natural precautionary equipment is somewhat out of control . . .

(That may seem an exaggerated example of the high anxiety that afflicts our family. Actually it's not much different from Miss Rose rushing up to filling stations in the middle of Kansas to ask if there are any mountains up ahead.)

Mac went to his work as usual; he had to do this. But he, too, was overwhelmed:

> TED: [Teddy (writing of himself in the third person)] remembered having heard as a small boy that his father was suffering from nervous prostration. He had been hopelessly puzzled by the term because, as far as he could tell, his father was walking around and behaving about the same as usual.

Teddy, too, experienced early glimmerings of the Great Fear.

> TED: Nor could he forget many long nights waiting on the porch—waiting and waiting and finally dashing through the darkness toward the bridge over to town in search of Mama and Dad who long since just ought to have been home.

(Waiting anxiously on the porch. Miss Rose does that every time she expects a family member to arrive.)

And the eighth grade morning when, for all his "bigness for his age," tears broke through Teddy's appeal to Dad to write a note asking Miss Ward to excuse him from reciting at the Friday afternoon exercises.

(Ted will suffer this fear of speaking in public for the rest of his life.)

Did the death of little Eleanor bring about this intense anxiety? Or did the Great Fear lie dormant within us until tragedy set its demons on the loose?

As MAC STARTED his thirty-first year with Labrot & Graham in 1911, both of the distillery's owners, James Graham and Leopold Labrot, died. The distillery came under the management of a son-in-law, passing over Mac. Sylvester Labrot, son of the former owner, offered Mac a position as manager of his creosote firm in New Orleans. If ever Mac were to enter a new line of work, here was the opportunity. With the tide of Prohibition running high, to stay in the whiskey business posed serious risks. *But creosote . . . ?*

Rose was weary of Kentucky's snowy winters when the house reeked of her children's wet woolens drying in front of the coal stove. Furthermore, by moving far away, she would be released from the ever-present reminder of little Eleanor, buried in the hilltop cemetery above Frankfort, and of her beloved father, who had died in 1898.

Mac went to look over the situation and wired Rose to come. Rose engaged two Pullman berths, put her French poodle in a basket underneath, and embarked with her children for *terra incognita*.

The *Frankfort Journal*:

> To the regret of their many friends, Mr. and Mrs. J. Mac Van Derveer and interesting family are expecting to leave soon for New Orleans, La., to make their future home . . . Mr. and Mrs. Van Derveer have been associated in the business and social life of the Capital for many years, and their absence will be keenly felt in the church and charitable work to which these good people have been so deeply interested . . . Their friends are loath to see them leave.

For white Southerners, privileged or plain, staying put is a virtual canon; moving away from one's roots, cousins, and connections, unless to marry into a wealthy Southern family, is deemed a grave lapse in judgment. By forsaking the Bluegrass, where their names were known, their looks a legend, their relatives a source of comfort and support, their friends only too willing to help Mac find a new livelihood, our family was to embody the folly of violating this unwritten law.

# PART TWO

# Before and After the First World War

*Scrapbook page of Dorothy in her
wedding dress, 1920; photo from the
New Orleans Times-Picayune.*

# New Orleans, 1912–1920

Fresh from the gray chill of Kentucky, the Van Derveers emerged into a strange tropical world of palm and banana trees, moss-hung oaks, oleanders, bougainvillea, crape myrtle, sweet olive, philodendron, and other exotic flora. Strangest of all in the midst of winter, they felt warm sunshine on their shoulders as they rode the St. Charles Avenue streetcar along this stately boulevard.

Mac engaged rooms at Mrs. Calder's boardinghouse on State Street. Rose, in particular, enjoyed the luxury of Mrs. Calder's five-course meals, served by white-coated waiters. Elizabeth, wide-eyed, pronounced:

*Swell!*

After supper on that first evening and many thereafter, Stewart and Teddy boarded the streetcar for the French Opera House on Bourbon Street. For college-age boys, admission to the third balcony was twenty-five cents.

Mac bought a house at 1429 Jackson Avenue in the Garden District. Rose shopped in the antique stores of Royal Street for Victorian settees, rosewood beds (to be draped in mosquito netting), washstands with heavy marble tops, and massive armoires (man-killers, complained many a mover).

They joined the Presbyterian Church; Mac sang in the choir. But Rose, having left New Thought behind her, surreptitiously slipped out of the Presbyterian fold to explore the philosophy advocated by Mary Baker Eddy, with its emphasis on the spiritual over the material. Not convinced by Christian Science, she had a brief fling with Unitarianism, being content to rely, at least temporarily, on reason and conscience.

Then summer set in. Hot! Natives had become acclimated or resigned to this fiendish heat. Or fled to summer homes in the Smoky Mountains, across the Lake,

*Rose and Mac at their New Orleans home, with windows open on a hot day.*

or along the Mississippi coast. In vain, Rose tried the local panaceas—fans, white slipcovers, grass rugs. Closing the windows made the house an oven; opening them admitted even more heat.

In July and August, the creosote works, where black workmen applied thick, hot oil to railroad ties, telephone poles, and raw lumber, became an inferno. Mac arrived home at night, still carrying the clean coat to his seersucker wash suit, his pants drenched in sweat.

Not only heat, but also hurricanes! In the midst of a hurricane, Mac struggled home, weary and wet. He decided, uncharacteristically, that one little toddy wouldn't doom him to eternal perdition. Exhausted, he fell asleep. Miss Rose, with her gift for hyperbole, reported by telephone to her brother, John, in Kentucky:

*Things down here are just terrible. The wind is howling, the palm trees are crashing down, the streets are covered with water. And Mac is stretched out on the couch, dead drunk!*

Lying far apart in their rosewood four-poster, Rose and Mac harked back in memory to the cool summer evenings of their courtship on Elkhorn Creek. Had their move been too hasty? Ill-advised? Motivated primarily by their desire to escape sad memories in Frankfort?

# The Baseball Pitcher

Teddy—as she always calls him—was Miss Rose's favorite child, almost embarrassingly so. Everybody noticed this; Miss Rose made no bones about it. She simply preferred men to women, beauty to ordinary, spirituality to horse sense.

Teddy—slender, tall, fair, blue-eyed—resembled Miss Rose's Stewart ancestors. He and his mother had in common their unusual beauty; in the glow of their youths, members of the opposite sex gawked—or swooned—at the sight of them.

Ted cannot have been unaware that he was extraordinarily handsome. On the Newcomb College campus, young women veered from their customary paths; on the St. Charles Avenue streetcar, they changed seats to get a closer look, perhaps even make the acquaintance of this gorgeous young man.

*Teddy in Navy uniform.*

COACHES AT TULANE University also took note of Ted; in 1913, an eighteen-year-old college boy standing six foot three was a rare bird. Ted played center on the varsity basketball team, one of eight regulars on a squad that won the state championship, inspiring Tulane's yearbook, the *Jambalaya*, to predict:

> We believe . . . basketball will now be a permanent sport at the university.

*Teddy, front row, left, on the 1913 Tulane University basketball team, state champions.*

Ted also became the star pitcher for the Green Wave baseball team. One afternoon, as practice ended, a member of the baseball team called to his teammate:

*Teddy, some fellow is here looking for you.*

That visitor delivered a bombshell: Ted's pitching statistics had come to the attention of none other than Connie Mack himself. Furthermore, Mr. Mack—as his players referred to him—had authorized the signing of Teddy to a contract with his Philadelphia Athletics, the team that had won the American League pennant and the World Series in 1910 and 1911.

Would Teddy consider such an opportunity? You betcha! Only days before the opening of the 1913 season, Teddy got a telegram from Mack instructing him to join the A's at Jacksonville, Florida, as they made their way north from Spring training. He began to pack his grip.

CONNIE MACK (BORN Cornelius Alexander McGillicuddy), the son of a mill worker of Irish antecedents, was one of two great baseball managers of the day, his rival being John J. McGraw, also of Irish working-class descent. Stocky, pugnacious McGraw always appeared in the New York Giants dugout in a clean uniform; in the heat of the fray, his language often became anything but clean. By contrast, gaunt, tall Connie Mack managed his Philadelphia Athletics clad in a dark business suit, complete with stiff collar, necktie, and stickpin; Mack never raised his voice to player or umpire.

Mack looked for prospects among college players. His search was rewarded, for example, with the famous pitchers Eddie Plank from Gettysburg College and Chief Bender from Carlisle Indian School, and the gifted second baseman, base runner, infielder, and left-handed batter Eddie Collins from Columbia University.

McGraw relied less upon college talent. But his ace right-hander Christy Mathewson, a graduate of Bucknell University, was well on his way to becoming one of the greats in the history of the game. In June and July, 1913, Matty pitched sixty-eight consecutive innings without walking a man, a record that stood until 1961. His matchless pitching arm, plus his model behavior, made

"Big Six" as his opponents called him, the first college graduate to become a major baseball star.

IN THE FIRST decade of the twentieth century, professional baseball was still a white man's game. Even the great Chief Bender, early in his career, heard the ugly chant:

*Get that Indian out of here!*

In 1911, the Cincinnati Reds, after signing two light-skinned Cubans, hastened to assure the fans that these newcomers were as white as Castile Soap. But the game remained barred to black Americans.

Connie Mack himself had once been humiliated by a desk clerk in a third-rate hotel in Washington, D.C., who refused to rent rooms to members of his team until they agreed to stay out of the dining room and not to mingle with other guests.

No matter how carefully Mack policed the behavior of his boys, despite the fame of college stars like Bender, Collins, Mathewson, and Plank, professional baseball was far from being regarded—particularly within the closed world of Philadelphia society—as a sport for gentlemen.

SOMEWHAT DUBIOUSLY, ROSE conveyed the news of Teddy's contract to her older sister, Bettie (called Auntie by her nieces and nephews), stern-faced, always clad in black in winter, the very embodiment of propriety on Philadelphia's socially exclusive Main Line. Bettie's husband, Dr. William Louis Rodman was a surgeon who had moved up the ladder of the rigidly conventional American Medical Association and was slated to become national president of that organization in 1915.

Auntie's reaction was unequivocal:

*Indeed not! McClellan is not to play professional baseball in Philadelphia!*

Auntie, a formidable figure even to Rose, prevailed.

*No, Teddy, you cannot accept that contract.*

*But Mama . . . !*

*Who could defy Auntie?*

ON LABOR DAY, as tradition required, male fans tossed their straw skimmers onto diamonds all over the country, demolishing this sweat-stained headgear and signaling the end of summer and the baseball season. Only the World Series, recently elevated to a national spectacle, remained to be decided. Could the A's become the first club to fly the World Series Championship pennant three times?

With Bender slated to take the mound for the A's and Mathewson for the New York Giants, fans of both teams anticipated a pitching duel between immortals. Both McGraw and Mack set great store on pitching; little boys worshipped pitchers more than hitters.

At the start of the third game, the Series was tied, one to one. McGraw had his great spitball pitcher, Fred Tesreau, fresh and ready for action. Mack, having already used Bender and Plank, was down to his pitching kids. Employing the eenie-meenie-minie-mo system, he chose Leslie Bush, a nineteen-year-old rookie from Butte, Montana, known as Bullet Joe.

Baseball being not yet available over the airwaves, Ted waited impatiently for the next day's *Picayune* to learn that Bullet Joe, by holding the Giants to five hits, had bested Tesreau and a second Giants pitcher and won the third game. In the game that followed, the A's clinched the Series, 3-1. Each Athletic drew $3,246, a bonanza in an era when an average player might draw $1,000 for an entire season and great stars like Ty Cobb and Honus Wagner earned only $12,000 and $5,700 respectively.

In years to come, Teddy often remarked wistfully that—had Auntie not put in her oar—he might have been the rookie pitcher of that third game.

TEDDY MUST HAVE hoped for a second chance. In the summer of 1914, he played in the bush leagues for the Gadsden Steelmakers. To celebrate the opening of the season, this small steel-producing town in north Alabama declared a half-holiday; fans jammed the streetcars headed for the ballpark.

On June 4, the *Gadsden Evening Journal* noted that the big man, Vandy, struck out nine, allowed only four hits, and thereby won a warm spot in the fans' hearts.

The Great Fear nowhere in evidence, Teddy enjoyed the excitement at the ballpark before he was to pitch a big game. He had good days and off days. When his pitching arm failed him, he tried to make up for it with his hitting. The *Evening Journal*, noting that Vandy had banged a triple, a double, and a single in four times at bat, headlined "VDV Loses Game but Stars with the Willow."

The lowly Steelmakers could not afford the luxury of players with a specialty, even pitching. During two months in Gadsden, Vandy played first base, second base, third base, center field, and right field. In one game, he pitched and later played right field; in another, he took turns playing right field and third base.

But no amount of effort could sustain the Steelmakers. Attendance dropped, especially on days when rain pelted the open stands. Disappointed fans subjected Vandy and his teammates to a rude chorus of jeers. When the Steelmakers fell to their arch rivals from Rome, Georgia, the *Evening Journal* reported: "The Romans hit Vandy whenever they pleased."

Teddy must have lost heart. No matter how high he leaped, he would never make the big jump from the Steelmakers to the Athletics or any other major league team. He would never get another shot at baseball immortality.

Connie Mack's star also faded. In 1914 the A's lost the Series to the Boston Braves in four straight. From 1915 through 1921, the A's finished last. The St. Louis farm system having caught on fast, Mack could no longer find the talented free agents that had once been so plentiful.

Vandy played his last game in Gadsden on July 13, 1914. He had a good excuse for leaving: Europe was on the verge of being engulfed in war. Even President Woodrow Wilson might not be able to maintain America's neutrality.

# The Ambulance Driver

Stewart strides down Birmingham's Nineteenth Street, bound for Alabama Power or Loveman, Joseph & Loeb, a batch of paper under his arm, tossing out cheery scraps of Italian:

*Buon giorno!*

*Come stai*

*Arrivederci!*

*A domani!*

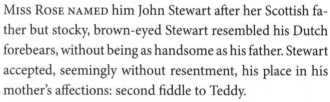

*Who's that Eye-talian fellow?*

*Oh, he's not Eye-talian. Drove an ambulance in Italy during the war.*

MISS ROSE NAMED him John Stewart after her Scottish father but stocky, brown-eyed Stewart resembled his Dutch forebears, without being as handsome as his father. Stewart accepted, seemingly without resentment, his place in his mother's affections: second fiddle to Teddy.

Rose and Mac proposed that Stewart become a doctor like his great-grandfather, Dr. Peter Van Derveer; his grandfather, Dr. Stewart; and his two uncles. They sent their first-born to prep school in Philadelphia, close to straightlaced Auntie and her husband, Dr. Rodman, the prominent surgeon.

But Stewart slipped away to attend concerts by John McCormack, Geraldine Farrar, and Enrico Caruso. Consumed by the idea of becoming a grand opera singer, he persuaded his parents to pay for voice lessons at the Philadelphia Academy of Music. Dr. Rodman strove to cure his nephew's romanticism but Stewart's case, as his life would prove, was incurable. After less than a year, he escaped Auntie's influence and rejoined his family.

WHY WASTE YEARS attending Tulane University when one plans to be an opera singer? In New Orleans, Stewart took more voice lessons, frequented the French Opera House, idled around Werlein's Music Store, appeared in a few comic operas, and spent his evenings managing the city's only filling station, located near St. Charles Avenue and Lee Circle close to the few families affluent enough to own an automobile.

In 1916, restless, doubtful of his prospects in opera, Stewart took off on what sounded like a grand, patriotic adventure. President Woodrow Wilson, provoked by repeated raids into Texas and New Mexico by the freebooting Mexican leader Pancho Villa, authorized General John J. Pershing to lead a punitive expedition into Mexico to pursue Villa. Wilson also called up 150,000 militia to be stationed along the border.

Stewart volunteered for this militia, joining Battery C of the Washington Artillery, the military pride of New Orleans. With some exaggeration, he described himself as an experienced horseman. In no time at all, he was in Donna, Texas, as official blacksmith and assistant to the veterinarian of Battery C.

Stewart spent nine months helping to guard the border. Nothing much happened. He represented his company in a boxing match against a professional boxer from another company (Stewart was knocked out) and got lost in the mesquite on a lone expedition to recoup a stray horse. During this tour of duty however, Stewart mastered one test of physical agility that he was to demonstrate on many occasions until his body lost its suppleness: he learned to walk on his hands.

*J. Stewart Van der Veer, oldest child of Rose Stewart and J. M. Van der Veer, ca. 1915 while under General Pershing, guarding the Mexican border against Pancho Villa.*

Weeks stretched into months without any hostile Mexicans in sight; the militiamen became bored. In January 1917, war with Germany imminent, Wilson withdrew the U.S. Expeditionary Force. Stewart and his fellow volunteers cheered the prospect of returning home.

STEWART, TWENTY-FOUR, AND Teddy, twenty-two, both unmarried—were prime candidates for the draft under the Selective Service Act of May 1917. Teddy, the minimum weight waived on his behalf, joined the Navy, eventually becoming a lieutenant assigned to serve out the war defending the unlikely target of Galveston, Texas. The Washington Artillery summoned Stewart back to active duty; he was dispatched to artillery training camp in Arkansas.

Both sons gone to war! Miss Rose found this unbearable. Of all her fears, the worst was that another death would occur within her immediate family, following the devastating losses of her sister, Eleanor, her adored father, and her baby daughter.

*Mac, you must sell this house!*

*Sell the house, Rose? Why ever for?*

*I cannot keep house with Stewart and Teddy gone to war!*

The Jackson Avenue house was sold, the massive furniture stored. Mac moved his family to what Elizabeth described as the swellest boardinghouse in New Orleans at 3218 St. Charles Avenue. All her needs attended to, all meals provided, Miss Rose was free to worry, day and night, until her sons came home.

STEWART, ON DUTY with a machine gun battalion in Camp Pike, Arkansas, experienced a mental and emotional crisis. He was nervous and depressed; he could not sleep; fears overwhelmed him. What caused this? Stewart and his father had different explanations:

Mac's letter to Stewart, New Orleans, February 11, 1918:

My Dear Boy:

　. . . My heart aches for you. You need not reproach yourself if you fail in anything . . . cut that fear of failure out . . . it is a mind condition . . . there is nothing for you to do but overcome your weakness by sheer force of will . . . even if you do fail in an examination or two. Many men have failed dismally and then pulled themselves together and won out . . . do brace up now, start at once and say you will banish this imaginary fear from your mind. I might tell you to resign your commission and come home but . . . far better if you were reduced in rank and stick it out . . .

But Stewart—even in old age when he has no reason to gloss over life's realities—

persisted in romanticizing his plight:

> STEWART (autobiography): The desire to see action on the front became an obsession. I requested transfer overseas several times, but it seemed that my group of officers was doomed to serve at Camp Pike throughout the war. I am constitutionally unable to weather prolonged frustration. It just gets on my nerves. My army doctor advised me to resign my commission and find some way to get overseas.

*Stewart, second from right, with fellow ambulance drivers, including, perhaps, Ernest Hemingway, left, on the Italian front, 1918.*

Did second lieutenants actually resign their commissions in frustration at not being sent to the front? Did Stewart suffer from nerves because he feared that he would fail some routine Army test? Or, deep in his subconscious, did he shrink from training men to kill? Did he fear that he himself would be forced to use a machine gun?

Stewart never examined the real cause for his attack of nerves; he did not wish to know.

> STEWART's letter to Mac, New York City, May 1918: Beginning to feel like myself . . . sincerely apologize for the anxiety and trouble that I have caused you in the past few months.

Stewart volunteered to become an ambulance driver for the American Red Cross. By going into the thick of battle, he would prove to skeptical friends that he did not resign his Army commission because he feared enemy fire. However, now he would be saving men, not killing them. Dispatched to Vicenza on the Italian front, he wrote his family faithfully, cheerful letters to his mother at the boardinghouse, the real stuff to his father at the creosote works.

*Stewart in uniform as a Red Cross ambulance driver.*

STEWART's letters to Mac:

JUNE 26: Was up under the big guns yesterday . . . well within range of Austrian artillery.

JUNE 28: As I was going into Italian trenches, had my first opportunity to see gas shells . . . An Austrian plane got over the lines this morning but our guns gave them hell.

JULY 8: I stood beside a trench mortar and watched them hurl shells into the Austrian trench which was about 100 yards distant across the river Piave. An Austrian machine gun was in action . . .

AUGUST 15: Have just returned from bombing practice behind the lines . . . hurled every species of bomb and hand grenade in the Italian army. Rather exciting work as some of them explode in five seconds . . .

AUGUST 25: Have now been shelled; some experience . . . shrapnel has bursted over my head . . . also a visit to no man's land . . . in other words I have received my baptism of fire . . .

OCTOBER 29: I know what hell is like now . . . all night long there was terrific bombardment over the entire front coupled with the machine guns . . . we slept in the car until a fragment whizzed by us . . . we had a bottle of wine along and this helped . . . to keep us from freezing stiff.

STEWART's letters to Miss Rose:

JULY 3: The Italians remark on my physique and think it uncanny that I know all of their operas perfectly.

JULY 8: On every occasion I have to sing the 'Prologue' [to *Pagliacci*] . . .

then they call 'bravo' and 'bella.' Every time I roll into a post I am hailed as the American Caruso and have to sing regardless of the surroundings.

AUGUST 25: Thank God for my knowledge of opera and ability to walk on my hands; you do not know how these little things help out over here.

AUGUST 28: Have just returned from a post where I was treated like a king. Every meal with the commanding colonel and attended the Golden Theatre with him every night . . . Had my own room with coffee in bed every morning . . .

SAVE MY LETTERS, Stewart pleaded; keep them in a bank box. The stuff he was writing in Italy, he said, would make a name for him. When the war ended, he was going to begin his career as a novelist.

Ironically, Stewart had a chance encounter with an acquaintance who would do just that. Upon meeting this tall, young man again, Stewart remembered only the nickname he bore at the training program for ambulance drivers in New York. Big Boy told Stewart he had quit ambulance driving and wangled an assignment as an informal, roving goodwill ambassador to Italian troops. He was on his way to the front lines to see war at close range. Someone had promised to take him that very night to a listening post barely fifty yards from the enemy lines.

Next day Stewart was summoned to help a seriously wounded patient whose leg has been shattered by a trench mortar. It was Big Boy. Stewart put his charge in a lower berth on the night train to Milan, took the upper berth himself, and saw to it that Ernest Hemingway was delivered safely to the hospital.

STEWART, July 12: In Milan for a couple of days. One of my squad caught a bomb the other night and was wounded rather severely. The Huns dropped a trench mortar shell into our trenches. I brought him in to the hospital here at Milan.

Here is how a real novelist, Ernest Hemingway—Stewart always insisted that Big Boy and Hemingway were one and the same—described this trip in *A Farewell to Arms*:

*The next day in the morning we left for Milan and arrived forty-eight hours later. It was a bad trip . . . We were sidetracked for a long time . . . and children came and peeked in . . . I got a little boy to go for a battle of cognac but he came back and said he could only get grappa . . . When it came, I gave him the change and the man beside me and I got drunk and slept until past Vicenza where I woke up and was very sick on the floor . . . Afterward I thought I could not stand the thirst and in the yards outside of Verona I called to a soldier . . . and he got me a drink of water . . . The soldier would not take a penny I offered him and brought me a pulpy orange. I sucked on that and spit out the pith and watched the soldier pass up and down past a freight-car outside and after a while the train gave a jerk and started.\**

# Marrying for Love and Beauty

### (Example 2)

I n the swarm of debutantes, gowned as brilliantly as peacocks for the Saturday night ball of the New Orleans Yacht Club during the Christmas season of 1919, one stood out. Teddy Van der Veer, recently home from service in the Navy, noticed her immediately. He asked his friend Gervais Favrot:

*Who is that girl in black?*

*Dorothy, left, 1919.*

Dorothy Rainold refused to make her debut, such unheard-of behavior attributed publicly to a recent death in her family. Her grandmother and step-grandfather, Captain and Mrs. Alexander M. Halliday, traveled to Boston to see her graduate from Wellesley College. En route home, they stopped in Cape May, New Jersey, to enjoy a few days of sea air. Diving from a platform, the famous steamboat captain hit an underwater stump, suffering a mortal wound.

Privately Dorothy explained that she declined to "come out" (in the old society sense) because she considered this a frivolous custom, a heretical notion she must have picked up during four years in the company of serious-minded New England females, practical young women from the Midwest, and the intellectual women who comprised Wellesley's faculty, most of them spinsters.

This grave, young woman charmed Ted. He confided his dreams of serving humanity and told her that he was searching for a life's companion with whom to spend evenings reading aloud, singing arias, exploring the meaning of life. Their courtship was brief and romantic; they became engaged at a performance of *La Traviata*.

Social scribes found certain aspects of the engagement unusual;

*Dorothy, left, Priestess from the South at Tree Day, Wellesley College, 1919. Courtesy of Wellesley College Archives.*

to their way of thinking, not altogether conventional. For one thing, the bride-to-be was not merely pretty:

*New Orleans Times-Picayune*: Beauty to Wed this Spring
    Within her lovely little head . . . there was a very brilliant brain, as proved by the fact that . . . she went to Wellesley where she graduated with honors.

    For another, she had not made her debut, owing, one writer explained, to mourning in the family. Furthermore, newspaper accounts made it plain that Dorothy had married outside the inner circle of New Orleans society:

    Mr. and Mrs. Van der Veer are delightful people, well-known in their own beloved native state of Kentucky.

*Dorothy, grave young woman, 1919.*

In other words, outsiders.

The bridegroom-to-be's prospects in life appeared somewhat vague:

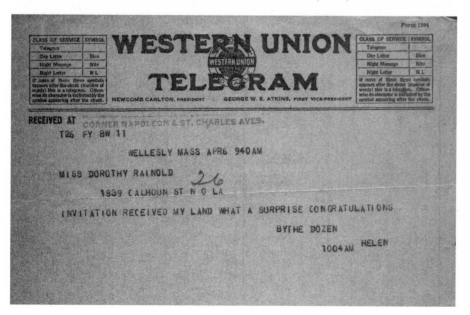

*Teddy, who could resist?*

> 'Teddy' is an unusually worthwhile, clever and attractive man . . . just now he belongs professionally to the *Item* where he has an important position on the editorial staff.

Less than a year after her graduation from Wellesley, Dorothy Rainold—hair bobbed, one curl on her forehead, wedding dress revealing her ankles—married Teddy Van der Veer in a home ceremony.

As had her mother-in-law, Dorothy chose a mate from the fringes of the current list of eligibles. Like Rose, she set her heart on a handsome suitor, prospects uncertain, family fortune nil; in short, she married for love and beauty, a romantic act that was to set Dorothy, as it had Rose, on an uncertain and wandering path.

She and Ted moved into the third floor of the big house at 4525 Prytania Street that Mac bought after the war. *(Taking shelter with the family.)*

*Wire from Wellesley.*

Form 1204

WESTERN UNION TELEGRAM

| CLASS OF SERVICE | SYMBOL |
|---|---|
| Telegram | |
| Day Letter | Blue |
| Night Message | Nite |
| Night Letter | N L |

If none of these three symbols appears after the check (number of words) this is a telegram. Otherwise its character is indicated by the symbol appearing after the check.

NEWCOMB CARLTON, PRESIDENT    GEORGE W. E. ATKINS, FIRST VICE-PRESIDENT

| CLASS OF SERVICE | SYMBOL |
|---|---|
| Telegram | |
| Day Letter | Blue |
| Night Message | Nite |
| Night Letter | N L |

If none of these three symbols appears after the check (number of words) this is a telegram. Otherwise its character is indicated by the symbol appearing after the check.

RECEIVED AT CORNER NAPOLEON & ST. CHARLES AVES.

T26 FY BW 11

WELLESLY MASS APR6 940AM

MISS DOROTHY RAINOLD      26

1839 CALHOUN ST N O LA

INVITATION RECEIVED MY LAND WHAT A SURPRISE CONGRATULATIONS

BY THE DOZEN

1004AM    HELEN

# Enid, Oklahoma, 1920

Ted grew up under the spell of the thunderous Henry Watterson, editor of the *Louisville Courier-Journal*. Years later, he told his friend and fellow newspaperman James Saxon Childers:

When Marse Henry spoke, the earth trembled. I knew he was the greatest man who had ever lived. I read everything he wrote. And I promised myself I'd be like him.

In Ted's day, people spoke of journalism as the newspaper *game*. No one ever spoke of the law game, the medical game, or the preaching game. Nor the banking game, the whiskey game, nor even the political game. The newspaper game was for those men who had been denied, by circumstances beyond their control, the formal education required to practice law or medicine or to preach from a Presbyterian or Episcopalian pulpit. And for those like Stewart and Ted with no inherited wealth or prominent connections.

Any fifth grade dropout, any three-pack-a-day smoker, an habitual drunkard, a victim of epilepsy—liable at any moment to fall from his seat on the rim of the copydesk in a grand mal seizure, spittle dribbling from his mouth—almost any clever wordsmith who could rattle the keys of a black Remington, using only his index

*Elizabeth, left, and Miss Rose meet a curious sight on a roadside near Enid, Oklahoma, 1921.*

fingers, or wield a fat, black pencil to compose headlines to fit an allotted space, could scratch out a living in the newspaper game.

For Ted, newspaper work was not a game; it was a calling. These flimsy black and white sheets were to be his pulpit. Through newspapers, he would spread knowledge, educate, serve. Ted rationalized, or really believed, that he could go to the library and read the great philosophers, Kant in particular, and thereby learn more than his Tulane professors could teach him. He dropped out of college.

He started his newspaper career in Kentucky in the city room of the *Lexington Herald*. After the war, he joined the ragtag band that produced the *New Orleans Item*. His colleagues were not filled with dreams of bettering the human condition. Some *Item* reporters even belonged to the Ku Klux Klan; one was a Kleagle. Another, a bootlegger. To augment their meager salaries, some took money on the side as press agents for dubious enterprises. Ted's friend Meigs Frost, quit the *Item*, hoping to break into the pulps that paid the munificent sum of $7.50 for a short story the same length as his daily newspaper column.

Nor did editors resemble Marse Henry. One stayed away from the office for weeks at a time; he was resting, he told his underlings; in an emergency, they could reach him at the New Orleans Country Club.

The only way Ted saw to achieve his calling was to own a newspaper. Stewart wanted to move back to the West; Rose found summers in New Orleans unbearable; Mac, hoping to please everybody, put up the necessary money for another family relocation. By now the family had a new member: Ted's twenty-two-year-old bride, the recent Wellesley graduate.

On January 9, 1921, the front page of the *Enid* [Oklahoma] *Daily News* carried a two-column photograph of a young man who looked more like a matinee idol than a newspaperman. The headline read:

McClellan Van der Veer Becomes Editor and Part Owner of The Enid Daily News.

*Elizabeth, in popular middy blouse, 1921.*

One word in that headline doomed this venture—the word *part*.

ELIZABETH, NINETEEN GOING on twenty, found herself yanked away from her Kappa Kappa Gamma sorority sisters and her classes in sewing and cooking at Newcomb College. Away from evening soirees at the Southern Yacht Club, tea dances at the Grunewald Hotel, parties aboard barges on the Mississippi River. Away from meals at Kolb's and Galatoire's. Away from Mardi Gras balls. Away from a cosmopolitan city where she watched stars perform at the Orpheum Theater, the "divine" Sarah Bernhardt reciting while seated on the stage because one of her legs had been amputated. Away from house parties at Pass Christian, dates with SAEs, KAs, Betas, and ATOs who drove big Marmons when they came home from Sewanee or the University of Virginia. Away from her first serious beau.

In 1921, Elizabeth found herself living in an old farmhouse ten blocks from the center of Enid, the only house for miles around with rooms big enough, ceilings high enough to accommodate Miss Rose's massive rosewood furniture. Writing a society column for the *Enid Daily News*. Going to plays and dances at the Elks Club, eating at the Enidine Cafeteria, or being offered at home strange dishes like chili by—of all things—a *white* cook.

*Leaving Enid: a bad day for driving.*

THE ENID VENTURE lasted a mere six months: Mac, Ted, and Stewart feared that the newspaper's circulation might have been watered, that is, falsely inflated. They could not—would not—do business in this manner.

# Kansas City, Missouri, 1921–1922

O ur family moved en masse to Kansas City—Ted, Dorothy (pregnant), Miss Rose, and Elizabeth by train; Stewart and Mac driving the Davis over muddy roads, getting stuck, being pulled out by men with mule-driven wagons. Ted, Stewart, and Elizabeth found jobs on newspapers, Stewart in advertising, Elizabeth writing Jane of Petticoat Lane, a shopping column.

*In Kansas City, 1921–22: top, Dorothy with Virginia; bottom, on a rocking horse.*

Miss Rose resumed her search for a religion to suit her needs; she tried out a famous preacher, Dr. Charles F. Aked, an ordained Baptist imported by John D. Rockefeller from England, who occupied the pulpit of the Congregational Church of Kansas City; Dr. Aked failed to satisfy Miss Rose. She had better luck at a nearby Unity Center; this movement, founded by Charles and Myrtle Fillmore, was akin to both New Thought and Christian Science. Unity espoused the concept that humans, through prayer and right thinking, could heal their physical and mental ills, regenerate their bodies, and attain eternal life. Right up Miss Rose's alley, so to speak.

I joined the family September 7, 1921. In years to come, I will often confront a faintly accusatory question:

*You're not from here, Virginia. Where were you born?*

At such moments, I am grateful, at least, for my narrow escape from Enid.

ELIZABETH WENT BACK to New Orleans to visit her friend, May; the visit was a disaster. She had bobbed her hair, the

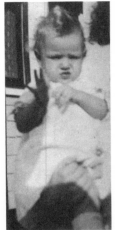

result: ruined! Her silk dresses, even her blue organdy with openwork lattice skirt, proved too hot for humid New Orleans; her old beaux, one by one, had been picked off for marriage.

Ted spent two years on the *Kansas City Post*, a morning paper controlled by Harry L. Dougherty, president of Cities Services Company, Kansas City's main public utility. He reported to the city room at 4 P.M., got home after midnight, just in time to hear the baby's fretful cries. Home being the third floor of Mac's big house at 3732 Valentine Road (Elizabeth always remembered house numbers).

But the *Post* was the wrong newspaper for a crusader; the *Star* was the major opponent of machine politics in Kansas City. The *Post*, a Democratic organ, supported Boss Tom Pendergast, who had built, through patronage and corruption,

the political machine that ran the city. Could an idealist make common cause with Pendergast? For Ted, the question answered itself.

Around this same time, another World War veteran, slightly older than Ted, took a more pragmatic view of life. This failed haberdasher launched his political career by running for eastern judge of Jackson County. Because he had the support of Boss Tom's brother, Mike Pendergast, Harry Truman was virtually a shoo-in.

*Holding grumpy*
*Virginia. Teddy,*
*above, tightly. Mac,*
*right, perilously,*

# New York City, 1923–1924

After the collapse of the Enid dream, fears began to overwhelm Ted. He feared that he would find himself accused of wrongdoing, possibly even in a criminal court. Suppose he should unwittingly be guilty of libel? Suppose he made a mistake in his income tax report? Suppose he hit somebody when driving an automobile? Suppose he had to undergo an operation? He supposed all these things and more. He hid these dark thoughts, even from Dorothy.

> TED: If anybody could know the kind of drivel that's going through my head, he would think I was crazy. Maybe I am . . . Anyway prison itself couldn't be any worse than all the torture I put myself through in being consciously and subconsciously afraid. I'm afraid something will separate me from Dorothy That's why I'm so afraid of death. I'm afraid of life without her. I'm afraid of death without her.

Ted decided to head for the mecca of American journalism. A strange move for a young man consumed by fear.

> TED: His hope of escape from intolerable apprehension had probably been the decisive factor in his coming to New York City. It was a move toward something greater . . . but it was also a desperate move . . . although he never quite made this explicit confession to himself.

He had no connections in this big-time newspaper game; he forced himself to go office to office, pleading for an interview. Before he was to spend a few

*Top, young New York residents Virginia and Dorothy. Below, Virginia (left) with friend, Central Park, 1924.*

minutes with some hardened editor, he ordered strong coffee to fortify himself. His hand shook; he could not hold the cup unless he propped his elbow on the counter. He swallowed the coffee so fast that he burned his tongue. While he talked to the editor, his heart beat so rapidly that he had to hold onto the city desk for support.

Eventually Ted got a job on the *New York Evening Post*. He was dispatched to his beat: a police station in lower Manhattan. Is this what he came to New York to write? Human interest stories of *les misérables* in a squalid police court? Most days nothing happened. Sometimes a week passed in which he got not a single telephone call from the city desk. Maybe they had forgotten him. He and a fellow reporter, Joe Cookman, whiled away the time debating whether God exists. Joe: definitely not. Ted, for the sake of argument, yes.

Landing a job in New York did not cure Ted's fears; everyday occurrences terrified him. For example, one of Dorothy's friends from her days at Wellesley asked Ted to give her away at her wedding. He quizzed Dorothy:

*Will there be anybody there?*

*Forty or fifty, perhaps.*

*And I'll have to march down the aisle with the bride before all those people?*

*Exactly.*

*How much does a giver-away have to say?*

*He merely says "I do" when the minister asks who gives the bride away.*

*You're sure that's all? Do you think I could march down the aisle without shaking so much that everybody will notice it?*

Ted's friend, Joe Cookman, was taken to a hospital suffering from the flu, often a fatal illness. Each night Ted got Dorothy to telephone the hospital; he could not endure the suspense of waiting for what message he might receive. He was reluctant to visit Joe; he got Dorothy and Virginia to walk to the hospital with him and wait while he went in.

Another of Dorothy's Wellesley friends had a sick child; Ted shut his ears to the problems of this child. He imagined that he himself had chest pains; would a heart attack soon follow?

He was transferred to City Hall. How splendid it would be, Ted thought, if he could make his stories about city government so penetrating, so illuminating, and so out of the usual rut of such reporting that he would be performing a real service to the people of New York. But the city editor had a different assignment for this greenhorn: stake out a millionaire's secret love nest and report who comes and goes. So this is how the *Evening Post* served humanity! Titillating readers with sex scandals. An older reporter advised Ted:

*Get out of this goddamned game. Get out and get out quick. You're too fine and clean to stay in this prostitution. It's filthy. It's vile. A man would be better digging ditches.*

*Virginia (right) and friend.*

Ted took the oldtimer's advice; he refused the assignment. His sympathetic editor proposed that he take a leave of absence but Ted had determined to quit. As a parting gesture, the editor offered him a week's pay. I can't take it, Ted said; I haven't earned it.

He rushed home to Dorothy:

*I'm done with that! I'm done, thank God, forever!*

He stayed home for a few weeks, resting, hiding. Finally, in the middle of a sleepless night, he awakened Dorothy:

*Sit with me awhile, will you. I've made up my mind. We'll call a doctor in the morning.*

For half an hour Ted kept himself busy getting ready. He bathed—getting into and out of the tub very carefully—remembering reading of people who had been found dead in the bathroom—shaved and dressed in his best suit. He must be prepared for whatever intimate rites the consultation called for . . .

For the first time in days he was conscious of feeling that he was doing something quite normal. Going to see the doctor. Everybody did that . . .

Ted and Dorothy sat on a lounge in the waiting room.

*"Well, I got here,"* he said in a whisper, speaking very rapidly. *"And I feel all right—better than I have for days. I guess I just needed some action."*

His heart was fluttering. His hands and feet were numbly icy. But he must talk. He couldn't merely sit. He might run and jump out that window—through glass and all. He had written a [newspaper] story once about a man who had thrown himself from a fifteenth-floor doctor's office . . .

God, just think of it! This doctor might say, "Nothing wrong with you much, my friend, you need a good rest and you'll be good as new," and then he could hug Dorothy and shout and cry for joy.

Or the doctor might say, "It's rather serious. I can't conceal that from you," meaning the very worst and then he would just sink to the floor at Dorothy's feet.

Either life or death. No man could be calm facing such alternatives! How silly to think that anyone with an iota of imagination and feeling could sit waiting for a verdict like this and not be overwhelmed by his helplessness, his pitiable agony of anxiety.

His brief mood of courage was gone. If that doctor did not hurry . . . and how would he act when finally he was face to face with the doctor? Would he be able to talk coherently or would he just cry out, *"Help me, please . . . help me!"*

# PART THREE

# Settling Down in Birmingham
## —The 1920s

## An Afternoon at Shadow Lake

*Left: "What's so funny about this, uncle?"*
*Above, at Shadow Lake bathhouse, Teddy*
*in back, next to Virginia and Dorothy, and*
*friends. Below, Virginia is the only child in this*
*family group, with Dorothy, left, and Elizabeth*
*in the water. Bottom left, a child in her wool*
*bathing suit (photo by Ed Willis Barnett).*

# Teddy's Child

Miss Rose fights against losing the only coin of her realm. She protects against wrinkles with broad-brimmed hats and veils, keeps her hands covered with white gloves, fluffs her bangs, blankets her face with powder, reddens her cheeks with rouge, and dyes (we used this harsh verb rather than "colors") her hair with some concoction of her own devising (food coloring? Easter egg dye? Or even, emulating women of ancient Rome who desired to be blondes, urine?). The result is any shade but white. Purple some days. Orange other days. Some days a mixture.

When Miss Rose was a belle, a famous surgeon, Dr. John Harvey Kellogg, superintendent of Battle Creek Sanitarium in Michigan, advanced the theory, along with a variety of other nostrums, that white clothing was better for the body than colored clothing. Miss Rose took Dr. Kellogg at his word. In an era when proper old ladies wear black—only black—in winter, Miss Rose wears white wool dresses, white wool coats, white wool hats. Where she obtains these almost unheard of items is a mystery. Perhaps a seamstress makes her dresses and coats to order.

So there we sit, Miss Rose and I, on occasional Sundays from November through February, in the third pew from the front at the fashionable Independent Presbyterian Church. Alabama's most famous preacher, Dr. Henry M. Edmonds, looking down from his high, carved pulpit upon dozens of white-haired women, is bound to notice the only one with purple hair. Not only that but, in a congregation garbed in various shades of black, the only one wearing white.

Dr. Edmonds thunders on, jowels quivering. This is the children's sermon; he is just getting warmed up for the main event. But can Dr. Edmonds maintain his stern expression when he notices what Miss Rose Van der Veer is up to now?

*Miss Rose's parlor photograph.*

Miss Rose does not believe in wasting valuable time: during the children's sermon, she deliberately rolls her blue eyes round and round in their sockets. After all, no one can see her but Dr. Edmonds. Suspecting that something unusual is going on, I sneak a sideways glance:

*What are you doing?*

*Ssh, Virginia. Listen to Dr. Edmonds. I'm just exercising my eyes.*

MISS ROSE KEEPS a large color photograph of herself prominently displayed in her front parlor. This photograph shows a much younger woman in a sleeveless crepe dress, with her hands clasped, a demure smile on her unlined face. When Elizabeth, Stewart, or, in later years, I, bring a new acquaintance to her house, Miss Rose invariably commands the visitor:

*Don't look at me now!*

Leading her puzzled guest to the parlor, she pulls the blinds, turns down the lights, and, gesturing to her picture, informs the newcomer:

*This is the way I really look.*

Her act makes an enduring impression. Half a century later, I run across childhood acquaintances who tell me:

*I remember Mrs. Van der Veer. She seemed so young; we couldn't believe she was a grandmother! And she always kept that beautiful picture of herself on her living room table.*

Naturally Miss Rose prefers this carefully posed studio photograph to those over which she has little control. But if she notices a Kodak Brownie aimed in her direction, she holds her head high, chin in air, to disguise, insofar as possible, any hint of double chin or crepey neck.

She is not keen on having her picture taken with me (likely to lead to embarrassing questions). She prefers to pose with Elizabeth's friends. On certain rural occasions, the Brownie captures one such group, Miss Rose in the center, as always. She is wearing a shirt, tie, and jodhpurs ("knickers") that show off her trim figure. When Elizabeth passes this snapshot around her office, strangers marvel:

*Elizabeth, is that really your mother?*

Elizabeth pays a price for her mother's fixation: celebrations of her birthday cease after she turns twelve. Miss Rose fears that all this loose talk about birthdays (How old are you, Elizabeth?) will lead to unwelcome speculation as to her own age.

To Miss Rose's way of thinking, two generations are enough

*Above, at Stewart's cabin, from left, Dorothy, Virginia, Miss Rose, Theresa Cory Strode, Lee Ola Shannon, unidentified woman. Below, Miss Rose, in summer white.*

for any woman to admit. Therefore, the fact that a four-year-old has joined her household poses a problem. It is simply too incongruous for the Belle of the Bluegrass—even at fifty-nine—to be publicly addressed as Grandmother, Granny, or Grandma. Or any other word with the syllable *gran* in it. Furthermore, she forbids me to call her husband Grandfather, Grandad, or Grandpa.

How to avoid such a clear indication of advancing years must have occupied her inventive mind in the dark reaches of many a night. Her solution is to require that I call her Mummy and her husband Daddy Mac or, simply, Daddy. If she thereby appropriated two terms that my parents might have liked for themselves, they will just have to settle for other forms of address. (I call them Uvvy, a failed attempt to say Mother, and Father.)

This matter resolved, there remains the issue of describing our relationship. If, for example, Mummy and I chance to meet an acquaintance on Twentieth Street:

*Why, Miss Rose, how nice to see you on this beautiful day. And this darling little girl. She must be your . . .*

Quicker than a wink, Miss Rose interrupts:

*This is Virginia.*
Then she offers her only explanation:
*Teddy's child.*

*Let Mac do the hugging.*

# A Turning Point for Teddy

Growing up, Ted believed that he was destined for great things. (Undoubtedly, Miss Rose encouraged this belief.) He was conscious of the rarity of his height and good looks. He assumed that his mind was as strong, powerful, and distinguished as his body.

TED: Since his boyhood, there had been a persistent though diminishing conviction in [Ted's] inner consciousness that eventually he was destined for the extraordinary. Was it possible that he should revise his estimate of his powers and limit his hope to a commonplace fate No! No! No! He was not ordinary. There were great powers within him!

But after the fiascos in Enid, Kansas City, and New York, Ted's faith in himself dwindled and its twin—fear—overwhelmed him. Now here he is in Birmingham, Alabama, dependent on the charity of his family.

TED TO HIS FRIEND JAMES SAXON CHILDERS: I set about looking at the snarl that had suddenly showed up inside me and separating and naming and understanding as far as I could the nerves and the ideas that had got themselves so tangled up . . . And it wasn't easy. There were days and terribly long nights when there was no separating or naming, and, least of all, understanding.

*Ted, worried.*

*Ted, in his time of trouble, 1925–29.*

TED OBEYS THE doctor's instructions: rest his mind; build up his body. After breakfast, he allows himself one of his daily allotment of five cigarettes. Glances over a New York newspaper to which he has subscribed. Helps Jerry, the man-of-all-work, with some simple task such as burning brush in the cow lot, fencing the chicken yard, planting the vegetable garden. Naps. Takes a short walk with Dorothy and Virginia, never far from the safety of home. After dinner, plays cards or works a crossword puzzle. Early to bed. Next day, the same. In calm moments, he assures himself that, in the ten days since their arrival in Birmingham, nothing has happened. Except his fear of what *might* happen.

# Going to the Picture Show

Ted, Dorothy and Stewart had to climb over a dozen men and women to get to their seats in the center of the third row of the Alabama Theater. Ted tried to arrange his long legs in the too-narrow space. He put his hat beneath his chair, folded his overcoat in his lap.

A comedy was being shown. He hoped it was near its end. His heart fluttered. His legs tingled. He tried another position, knees propped against the seat in front. How enormous was the woman to his right! Suppose he had to get out quickly? What a job it would be squeezing past those billowing knees! What would she and all the others, over whom he would have to climb again, think? They would think he was just plain crazy, climbing in and out over people right in the middle of a show.

To hell with them! He would go if he wanted to. He got out his handkerchief and wiped the perspiration from his forehead. God, how stuffy it was! If only that woman did not bulge until her shoulder pressed softly, hotly, against him.

*Don't you think it's awfully close in here?* he whispered to Dorothy.

*I hadn't noticed it,* she replied.

He had two hours of this to go through? Hadn't the doctor said he must stop forcing himself to do things? Here he was, with his wife and brother, out to enjoy himself as hundreds were doing, their laughter furnishing the evidence. And he was quivering and sweating and tingling. About what?

His heart thumped and skipped. The sweating would not stop. And something in his legs was leaping like his heart.

God, he couldn't stand it another minute! The doctor had said, don't fight it now, give in, it takes too much of your strength to fight it now.

He was surprised at his voice. It sounded quite normal and controlled.

*I've got to go out for a while. I'll either come back or wait for you at the Tutwiler Hotel.*

*Shall I come with you?* Dorothy asked, unable to conceal her anxiety.

*No, I'm quite all right.*

He must go now. They couldn't have a debate in the theater. Everybody would be listening. He felt better now that he was moving, even though he imagined the glare on the fat woman's face.

He found a vacant seat near the fireplace at the Tutwiler. What had happened? He couldn't, now that he was calm again, explain what it was that had made him want to go. That overpowering impulse to go—there was no forgetting that, even if there were no explaining it . . .

# Walking Home from the Car Line

The drug store was open but the solitary clerk looked lonely. Ted and Dorothy walked past the last city lights and the last gasoline station. First Avenue became a country road and stretched into the darkness.

The sky was black smoke. Ted felt scattered drops of rain on his face. His body seemed to be swaying gently from side to side. He took Dorothy's arm. That helped. He would talk to her and get his mind off himself. His whole trouble, that was. His mind always on himself.

He seemed unable to keep from walking off the edge of the road onto the uneven gravel. If he should collapse, what would Dorothy do? It might be long minutes before an automobile came along. His steps were getting more and more uncertain. A sudden impulse to start running as fast as he could flashed through him. No, he couldn't do that. Dorothy couldn't run. Anyway he would soon fall flat on his face.

An automobile was coming. He had better stop it. He could simply say he was not feeling well. But the driver might think he was going to be held up. The car sped past.

The road seemed to become perpendicular, a wall in front of his face. He could go no farther. He stopped.

*Dorothy, I've got to rest a minute.*

He tried to control his voice so she would not suspect. And it might pass. He had felt like this in New York on Columbus Avenue. That had passed.

He clung to her arm. His trembling communicated itself to her.

*Ted, you're shaking! What's the matter? You must sit down. Right here. Here's a big rock. Hadn't I better run to one of those houses and get somebody?*

*No. I was this way before once. It'll pass.*

He didn't want her to leave him. It might not pass. He didn't want to be alone if it didn't.

*I'm feeling better. I can get up now.*

*Give me your hand. I'll pull you up.*

He took her arm and, slowly, they trudged on. One step at a time finally would get them there. And if he had to, he could sit down again . . . "

EXISTENCE WAS A process of getting through hour by hour. Sometimes minute by minute . . . He knew now the full potentialities of his predicament: life or death, sanity or insanity.

Scarcely an hour passed when he was free from the feeling that any minute might bring a panic of his entire being from which he might never emerge. He might palpitate and tremble into death. He might fear and fear until he could fear no more and his mind was gone.

LEANING ON HIS rake, watching the brush burn, Ted tries to figure a way out of his predicament.

> TED: Maybe it is intended that the power that is given you shall run down. And that it shall be up to you to make power for yourself. Maybe whatever it is that is "you" is capable of creating health to go with a mind that can decide and a spirit that will not quail.

Maybe I can do something about it, Ted thinks to himself. At least, for the sake of Dorothy and Virginia, he must try. Ted has not been downtown since the dark night he and Dorothy struggled home from the Loop. He must try to walk this short distance alone. But no sooner is he out of sight of his parents' home than fear takes over. If I turn back now, Ted says to himself, I will have given in again to the fear.

He picks out a tree ahead. If he can get that far . . . he does. He sets his sights on another tree. One tree at a time. Finally he reaches the Loop and a waiting streetcar.

> TED: It seemed to him as if the streetcar were barely moving. He was

acutely afraid he might have to get off . . . he was perspiring again. It was very stuffy . . . And then, quite mysteriously—all his emotions and feelings *were* so mysterious, so independent of reasonable cause—he realized that he was not going to have to get off of the car! He wouldn't have to sit on the curb and then maybe have to telephone Dorothy to come and get him. He was going to town.

After that small triumph, Ted goes into town each weekday. He runs little errands, delivering jobs to customers of the Van der Veer Company, his family's advertising agency, forcing himself to make light conversation with receptionists. A handsome man, not yet thirty, who once believed that he was destined for the extraordinary, reduced to an errand boy. Then one banner day he lands an order from Loveman, Joseph & Loeb, Birmingham's leading department store.

TED REALIZES THAT he has another problem: he is too dependent upon Dorothy. She had married a seemingly confident man. How could she love one so crippled in spirit? One evening, as they sit by the fireside, Ted proposes that Dorothy pay a visit to her grandmother in New Orleans, taking Virginia with her. And she will have to stay until he proves that he can deal with his fears on his own. Reluctantly Dorothy consents.

Three months pass. Ted gains a little more confidence each day. He desperately wants to be reunited with his wife and daughter. But first, he steels himself to pass one more test: he must spend a week alone, miles away from his parents, brother, and sister.

On his first night in an isolated cabin on a mountaintop in northeast Alabama, Ted imagines that his heart is skipping erratically:

> TED: He might just die here on the mountain, away from Dorothy, away from everybody. Couldn't Stewart see that he was in no condition to go out into a wilderness alone? All his struggling to come back, all his agonies gone for nothing. His life to end in a fool's death on a mountain top . . .

He imagines himself running wildly through the woods, crying and shouting to Dorothy. But he cannot possibly reach Dorothy, hundreds of miles away.

Snap out of it, Ted tells himself. You've been through this same old stuff so many times before.

Finally the terror subsides; he sits outdoors on a log and lights a cigarette. Somehow, he resolves, he will manage to hold a job. But no matter what the job, Ted vows to hold fast to his ideals and convictions. He will not allow these to be taken away from him.

Then he goes into the cabin and to sleep.

Next morning Ted walks seven miles to a little village. He telephones Dorothy. He is going to pass his test on the mountain, he tells her; then it will be time for her to return.

*Snowy front and side views of Topside.*

TED AND DOROTHY buy a few acres on top of a hill about a mile from Miss Rose's place. They build a tiny house—one bathroom, two bedrooms, living room, dining room, kitchen. No furnace. A one-car garage with a room and bath in the rear that we refer to as the "servant's quarters." It never occurs to us to connect the term "quarters" with backyard cabins of slavery. Where in the world did we get a few hundred dollars for this venture? Dorothy's wealthy grandmother—the one who had paid for her Wellesley education—died about this time. Perhaps there was a small inheritance. After living under Miss Rose's roof for so many years, Dorothy must have seen this as, literally, manna from heaven.

Ted gives his home a name harking back to his days in the Navy: *Topside*. He sets in to create his own little world, peopled by those who spend their evening listening to *La Traviata* or reading aloud and their Sunday afternoons protecting home plate with the bases loaded. Roebuck Springs has already attracted a smattering of writers who make up Birmingham's only approximation of a bohemian group. Ted wants to build on this small base: congenial neighbors, sharing a love of sports, music, reading, and high-minded thoughts.

HE STILL HAS occasional bad spells, disappears into his bedroom. Uvvy tells me to be quiet—Father has a headache.

After he comes home on the streetcar from a long day of striding up and down Nineteenth and Twentieth Streets, Ted sits down at his typewriter. He is trying to exorcise The Great Fear by writing about it in the form of a novel.

> ELIZABETH: We were at Ted's until 1:30 A.M. reading his opus. It's long and heavy in his usual manner and style so I don't know what to say about it.

(Well, Elizabeth, you could say that Ted's novel is based on stark, unadorned truth.)

# Shelter from the Elements

Summer. We live in the country. Roads unpaved. Houses far apart. Dense forest pressing in on all sides, providing some relief when the temperature soars above 100 degrees for five days in a row, reaching 107 degrees in 1930, a record that is to stand throughout the twentieth century. Even Elizabeth complains mildly to her diary:

Boy, has it been warm!

Cicadas drone; the warmer the day, the louder the sound. Doves utter their plaintive calls. Lightning bugs wink in the early darkness. Crickets and katydids hum like a giant harmonica. Tree frogs trill. If I run fast enough from tree to tree, I can stop their noise, briefly. From deep in the woods, an occasional seductive call:

Whip-poor-will!

*Hush, everybody, listen for the whip-poor-will.*

From the other side of Ruffner Mountain, locomotives hoot and moan as they pass through Irondale and Woodlawn, their engineers warning the rare pedestrian or motorist. Or simply greeting fellow travelers on this lonely track. Late in the night, we hear owls asking:

Who? Whhhho?

On hot evenings, we sit on Miss Rose's big, open porch, praying to catch a breeze. Well, not literally praying, just hoping.

Fall. I decorate the living room with armloads of the goldenrod that flourishes, unbidden, in fields and along roadsides; it sheds little petals over the Oriental rug. Uvvy decrees: no more goldenrod, Virginia! Go pick some chrysanthemums from the garden.

Friends from town come to call, bringing two mischievous boys about my age. As they leave, one boy throws a chestnut bur; it hits my cheek. While I weep, Uvvy uses tweezers to remove a lot of little sharp spurs. She never tells the other mother about this; it wouldn't be polite.

Winter. Not as mild as Mac envisioned when he looked on the map and saw how deep this young city lies within the South. Occasionally a heavy snow blankets its streets and roads. Birmingham does not own a single piece of snow-moving equipment; no use shelling out money for an expensive machine to deal with what may be the only snow of the winter. Just leave it to the big streetcars that run up and down the valley to clear their tracks and convey office workers and department store clerks downtown. With no shoppers or customers in sight, most stores and offices close by mid-afternoon. Residents of hilly streets have little choice except to stay put. Miss Rose never fails to gloat:

*Aren't you glad we don't live over the mountain!*

> Elizabeth: Cold walking to carline. I started out at 7:30 a.m., galoshes, socks. Waited 20 minutes for streetcar . . . creeping to town. Got there about 9:30 a.m. Few calls and no visitors. There won't be many at the President's [Franklin D. Roosevelt] birthday ball tonight. I'll never forget this Christmas with its terrible weather. (Snow, sleet, rain and below freezing for almost two weeks now.)

Streetcars number twenty-five and number thirty-eight (five cents each way to downtown and back) are our lifelines of escape from the winter blues.

> Elizabeth: Mama and I went to town on the streetcar in the third snow of the winter to see Katherine Hepburn [in *Morning Glory*].

Miss Rose's big house, built as a country retreat from the heat of summer, has fifty-seven windows and no insulation. No matter how much coal Mac and Stewart shovel into the always ailing furnace, the interior remains almost as frigid as the icebox on the back porch. They give up trying to heat the whole house.

Miss Rose and Mac are free, if they choose, to create warmth in their double bed. But having long since outlawed sex, Miss Rose keeps her double bed for

*Fifty-seven windows and no insulation.*

convention's sake. (Or so I surmise.) A small anteroom adjoins their bedroom; it holds a daybed just barely long enough for me when I spend the night. Also, I suspect, for frequent use by Miss Rose herself.

Stewart and Elizabeth put on heavy bathrobes and retreat to the faint warmth of their closets; I hear the clatter of typewriter keys.

WORSE THAN SNOW, winter rains, ugly and confining. Elizabeth and I are bored to distraction.

> ELIZABETH, January 1936: It has rained constantly since daylight and we are all housebound (Everyone discussing Roosevelt's speech and the death of the AAA [The Agricultural Adjustment Act invalidated by the U.S. Supreme Court].

> VIRGINIA: I'm so sick of rain I could scream. There hasn't been a bright day since Christmas.

Housebound. How to pass the time? Play long, dull games of Chinese checkers. Join Mac and Stewart to listen to "Amos 'n' Andy" on the radio. Read (Elizabeth) *The Forsyte Saga* and *Jalna*; (Virginia) *The Last of the Mohicans* and *Black Beauty*.

Or draw chairs close to the fireplace and retell old stories about our forsaken Edens, tongues almost caressing the syllables:

Kentucky: the Pendennis Club. Ver-sails. Lexington, Owensboro. Simon Bolivar Buckner. 'Desha Breckinridge. Birdie Brown. Hen'retta Blackburn.

And tales like the one about Lily knocking on the door of Rose's bedroom on the morning after her wedding. Or Stewart's recollections of peeking at the painted girls from Minnie Bell's Place in Gas House Alley when they occupied their usual front-row seats in the balcony of Frankfort's Opera House . . . and stumbling upon a rowdy picnic at Elkhorn Creek where he saw German glass-blowers with big chests and women clad only in kimonos.

Elizabeth recollects a clear, wintry night in 1910 when her father carried her to the steps of Kentucky's new Capitol, with its broad vista of night sky, and instructed his nine-year-old daughter:

*Look up!*

Mac wanted Elizabeth to remember, as she always did, that she had seen Halley's Comet.

I've heard all those stories many times but—"Amos 'n' Andy" not being on the radio tonight—I listen again. Perhaps things will turn out differently this time; maybe one of those women picnickers will slip out of her kimono; maybe Halley's Comet will graze the Capitol dome; maybe the man in Rose's bedroom wasn't Mac after all; maybe it really *was* John McDowell.

The storytelling locale switches to New Orleans: The exotic names of streets and avenues . . . Napoleon . . . Prytania . . . Tchoupitoulas. Their schools: New-comb, Tulane. Their friends: Ves' Labrot . . . Gervais Favrot . . . Meigs Frost . . . "Winkie" Barr.

Finally, my elders speak of their faraway relatives . . . Auntie and Cud'n Mary Yandell in Philadelphia . . . Aunt Minnie and Uncle John in Frankfort. Where they *belong*.

During long rainy spells, tensions mount, there being little or no sex to clear the air. On one occasion, Mac gets mad because Stewart brings fish home for dinner and smells up the house. After a while, nobody remembers what started these fights.

Red-faced, bloated with anger, Stewart appears at *Topside* to spend a night or a week. He and his father stop riding to town in the same car; the partners in the Van der Veer Company take the streetcar to work, each in a window seat. Mac falls silent for long periods; at the office he refuses to work. No one recognizes these symptoms as signs of depression.

Teddy, Dorothy, and I also live in an uninsulated frame house. *Topside* has no furnace at all. In the living room, we make do with a big coal stove and a large fireplace; on cold mornings, I dress behind the stove. Each bedroom has a small fireplace with a coal grate. Dorothy and Ted warm one another in their double bed, taking care to keep the sexual flames low. They are determined that one child is enough.

Huddled under piles of blankets, I love to watch the firelight flicker on my bedroom walls, dimly illuminating the print of a demure, barefoot girl, seated, hands clasped (Sir Joshua Reynolds's *The Age of Innocence*, my mother's selection), and lending a touch of reality to the picture of a sunset that I made myself out of red and blue tinfoil.

This little pile of coals never lasts the entire night. One morning I wake up to the sight of my two goldfish, bought at Woolworth's, strangely stiff and unmoving in their small bowl, a glaze of ice on top. I scream for our cook:

*Audrey, come quick!*

*Lord mercy, child, them fish done froze!*

Spring. At last, spring releases us from isolation. Seductive spring. Roebuck is ablaze with color . . . dogwood, redbud, apple, and plum trees in full regalia. Yellow jonquils, purple flags, blue hyacinths.

I wander about the woods by myself; Dorothy has no fears for my safety. I suck the sweetness out of a honeysuckle stem, bury my nose in the pollen of buttercups to make a clown's face, pick bouquets of purple roosterheads and smaller, darker violets, pink Sweet William, and tiny, yellow star flowers. I take these offerings to Uvvy (as soon as they show the first sign of wilting, she tosses them out in favor of bouquets from her garden); I gather entire baskets full of wildflowers to present to neighbors and friends on May Day.

Our house is open to other living creatures. In my closet, I find a strange, diaphanous rope draped over my dresses.

*Audrey, come quick!*

*Lord mercy, child, some snake's done shed his skin!*

# Miss Rose's Place

In our neighborhood a few old families, who refuse to move to fashionable new developments over the mountain, cling to their big country properties, several of which boast their own spring-fed, small lakes.

Perhaps remembering the summers of her courtship at Elkhorn Creek campground, Miss Rose assumes at first that these little swimming holes belong to the entire community. She leads Elizabeth, Dorothy, and me to the one nearest her house. Just as we are summoning up the courage to dip our toes in its frigid water, an irate owner appears to set us straight. We trudge home on the hot, dusty road, Elizabeth and I disappointed, Miss Rose indignant, Dorothy mortified.

Miss Rose, Mac, Stewart, and Elizabeth live in a large two-story cottage of the Arts and Crafts style popularized around the turn of the twentieth century by William Morris and Gustav Stickley. This house is located—at Miss Rose's insistence—in the valley.

Miss Rose adorns her living room with a Van der Veer crest that she ordered through the mail, with its smug motto, *Aut Inveniam, Aut Faciam* (what we start, we finish), a photograph of her brother John Stewart's big home in the Bluegrass, a sketch by Paul Sawyier of an old bridge at Frankfort, two Currier and Ives prints, and, in the place of honor, her this-is-the-way-I-really-look photograph. Over the big stone fireplace, a plaster of Paris lion's head, with empty eyes, gazes mournfully down. Adjoining the living room is what she calls the music room, with its Kurtzman upright piano and a small stand especially designed to hold sheet music.

A downstairs bedroom is consecrated for rare use by visiting relatives, most often Miss Rose's older sister, Bettie, from Philadelphia. This badly needed space—and bathroom—is off-limits to the regular occupants of Miss Rose's house.

*Miss Rose's place in late fall.*

When Auntie, with her stout figure, white hair, and black dress, alights from the Pullman of the Birmingham Special, she takes one look and begins to scold:

*Oh, Rose!*

Auntie is the only family member with the temerity to try to change her younger sister's taste in clothes, hair, politics, eating habits, and manner of life. Her husband, Dr. Rodman, had indeed served as president of the American Medical Association in 1915-16; that gave Auntie a certain authority.

Auntie usually stays a month. I hear her fervent expression of shock and dismay a lot.

Elizabeth: Auntie and Mama had many little tiffs.

Miss Rose is not about to relinquish purple hair, white wool dresses, pacifism, salmon croquettes, or her search for the Fountain of Youth. She gives Auntie back as good as she gets:

*Bettie, let me be!*

Miss Rose, Mac, and their middle-aged offspring occupy three upstairs bedrooms and share one bathroom. Unlike her bedroom in Enid, Miss Rose's bedroom on Exeter Drive is big enough for the massive rosewood furnishings she chose on Royal Street, the four-poster bed, two dressers, marble-topped washstand, and armoire having miraculously survived trips aboard freight trains from New Orleans to Enid to Kansas City to Birmingham.

This house is surrounded on two sides by a deep porch large enough for an assortment of rocking chairs and a table for pingpong; Elizabeth enjoys her status as family champion. In one of these porch chairs, I—age four or five—am rocked to sleep by Miss Rose. When my parents are invited to dinner at friends' homes, I always spend the night with Mummy, the practice of paid babysitting being unheard of.

In her soft, sweet soprano—the voice of Pitti-Sing long ago—Miss Rose sings lullabies from her own childhood and bedtime songs she sang to her children. She begins briskly, with my favorite:

> Dance the boatmen, dance
> Dance the boatmen, dance
> Dance all night in the pale moonlight
> And go home with the girls in the morning.

Miss Rose does not realize that these lyrics refer to rough men who guided flatboats, loaded with charred barrels of corn whiskey, down the Ohio and Mississippi Rivers to New Orleans, then turned around and walked all those miles back home. She might not have sung it to me if she had the faintest notion of the implication behind the words "And go home with the girls in the morning." The boatman song is followed by a wistful ballad:

> Go tell Aunt Nancy
> Go tell Aunt Nancy
> Go tell Aunt Nancy
> Her old gray goose is dead
>
> The one she's been saving
> The one she's been saving
> The one she's been saving

To make a feather bed.

Then, inevitably, songs by Stephen Foster. Practically every minstrel troupe that visited Frankfort when Miss Rose was a belle presented "Old Black Joe" and other tunes in which Foster used words like darkey and nigger. But Miss Rose and I are so caught up in the story of "Old Uncle Ned," whose master cared for him and wept when he died, that we do not even notice Foster's racist terms.

> There was an old nigger
> And his name was Uncle Ned
> And he lived long ago, long ago
> And there warn't no wool
> On the top of his head
> In the place where the wool oughta grow

Miss Rose concludes her little bedtime recital with a song by the lesser known B. R. Hanby. She has no idea that "Nellie Gray," popular in the North during the Civil War, is about a slave mourning that his loved one has been sold; Miss Rose only knows that this melody lulls me quickly to sleep:

> Oh My Poor Nellie Gray
> They have taken you away
> And I'll never see my darling anymore
> I'm sitting by the river and I'm weeping all the day
> For you've gone from the old Kentucky shore

(I remember these plaintive lullabies so vividly that, seven decades later, I will sing to my own grandchild, with certain words changed, about the rowdy boatmen, the dead goose, old Uncle Ned, old Black Joe, and poor Nellie Gray, sold away.)

# Stewart's Place

Stewart is a bachelor. This is not—as in the case of some of Elizabeth's beaux—society's polite cover for homosexuality. Stewart is simply an unmarried man. No one, however, speaks of Stewart, edging toward forty years of age when the Great Depression slams into us, as an eligible bachelor. Stewart lives, as he always has, with his mother, father, and sister. He hasn't a spare dime to his name. Any sensible young woman can see at a glance that Stewart is an *in*eligible bachelor.

Stewart loves to spend Saturday afternoons and Sundays puttering around Miss Rose's place, taking care of three hounds, a cow, some chickens, two horses that he boards, and his own horse. He teaches me to ride after a fashion (or un-fashion), safe inside one of his big Western saddles, clinging to its tall pommel, jouncing until I learn to post. I ride with Stewart to the blacksmith shop at Huffman to watch the sparks fly and marvel at the stoic horses as the blacksmith pounds nails into their hooves.

*Left, Virginia on Stewart's horse, Blaze; right, Elizabeth and Stewart.*

*Stewart's cabin, Shadow Lodge.*

But Stewart does have a place of his own. Not, like Miss Rose's big house, a shelter filled with hidden tensions. Not, like our small house, a place for Ted to hide when his inner torments become unbearable. Stewart's place exists solely for fun.

His neighbor, Chappell Cory, takes a liking to Stewart and allows him to build a cabin on the Corys' land far out in the country. Stewart rides his horse to his cabin, a leisurely journey of about seven miles along a dirt road lined with honky-tonks. The rest of us make this trip in our black Ford.

Stewart names his place *Shadow Lodge*—a bit grandiose for a one-room log structure with a little shed porch and an outhouse. We call it simply Stewart's cabin. It sits close by Turkey Creek, a meandering stream noted for the number of stills that line its banks to make illegal use of its clear spring water. I dip my bare feet in the icy Big Spring where Stewart gets his drinking water; my toes turn pink and the chill spreads to my shoulders. I wade on the smooth rocks and slippery moss of Turkey Creek.

Sometimes I spend the night in one of Stewart's hard bunks. I love to watch the flickering red flames die down in the little stone fireplace, smell the smoky aroma of the log walls, and listen to the rustle of Turkey Creek. If I stay awake late enough, I can hear bullfrogs croak and owls hoot.

WHEN THEY ARE not at their place on Turkey Creek, the Corys are at their more formal home across the road from Miss Rose's place. Chappell Cory is something of an itinerant newspaperman himself, albeit well-connected. His wife, Marielou, who worships the memory of Jefferson Davis, frequently travels to Montgomery to serve as a hostess at the first White House of the Confederacy.

The Corys' daughter, Theresa, is about Elizabeth's age. There the resemblance ends. When Theresa lets her black hair hang loose to her waist, she looks like those bare-breasted South Seas women whose pictures I see in *National Geographic*. (Theresa does not bare her breasts; at least not in public.) When she twists that shiny hair into a big, fat coil, Theresa might almost be taken for what we call an Oriental. Except for her pop eyes. I overhear Stewart talking to Elizabeth about Theresa's *bedroom* eyes; what could that mean?

Living so close, one would think that Stewart and Theresa would take at least a passing fancy to one another. But Theresa sets her bedroom eyes on bigger game; a successful writer, Hudson Strode, who teaches at the University of Alabama in Tuscalooa. By golly, she lands him!

About a week before their wedding, the Corys' house burns to the ground. Mrs. Cory implores the neighbors and the firemen to save Theresa's wedding presents. Even more important, save her trousseau (all those hand-embroidered, lace-trimmed, silk and satin intimate garments)!

With his hunting boots, Stewart stamps out the last little tongues of flame.
*Come on to our house Miz Cory. It's too cold to stay out here in the dark.*
Mrs. Cory keeps poking in the ashes.
*What you lookin' for, Miz Cory?*
*Something I've just got to find!*
*What's that, Miz Cory?*
*My UDC\* pin!*

Theresa and Hudson marry in a little private chapel built by the Ross Smith family during Roebuck's palmier days. The temperature that night is twenty degrees; inside Wilson Chapel, thanks to a few candles and body heat provided by the guests, it rises to one or two degrees above freezing. Outside a bunch of roughly dressed men gather. Their horses, nostrils emitting warm breath like little white puffs of smoke, let out impatient neighs and paw the ground. His friends are waiting for Stewart to emerge from the chapel. Then they will head for Turkey Creek; it's a perfect night for a possum hunt.


HUDSON DOES NOT approve of his wife's plain, country name. So he "Frenchy-fies" it: Thérèse (pronounced Tuh-rez). We find it hard to remember to say Tuh-rez instead of Theresa.

Hudson and Thérèse travel the world; he writes books about Mexico, South America, and other faraway places. They spend an entire year in Scandinavia, get acquainted with Isak Dinesen (Baroness Blixen) and Sigrid Undset, the 1928 Nobel Prize winner. In New York City, Hudson charms publishers and inveigles them to publish the work of his students. In the waning years of his life, Hudson will even give in to Marielou's pleas and write a biography of Jefferson Davis.

Meantime Stewart seldom leaves Birmingham, squeezes a bare living from the family advertising agency, publishes a few Western stories and three potboiler

*\*United Daughters of the Confederacy*

novels. As to a husband, Thérèse has made a wily and, from her standpoint, wise choice. Still she keeps in touch with her former neighbors.

Thérèse comes to dinner at our house; her hair shines, she laughs coquettishly. Uncharacteristically, Father also laughs a lot that evening; he seems unnaturally gay (in the 1930s connotation), not his usual, sober self. Even I, innocent of all innocents, realize that Thérèse is giving off an aura that seldom, if ever, pervades our house. I sense that it poses some sort of threat to my mother.

> ELIZABETH: Thérèse Strode spent Labor Day weekend with us. She and I didn't get along so well . . . we're so far distant in ideas and objectives . . . I was violently ill to my stomach before the visit was over.

TURKEY CREEK FEEDS a little swimming hole that Mr. Cory has named Shadow Lake [*see photos, page 58*]. He invites our family to swim there. As boys in Kentucky, Stewart and Ted swam in the Kentucky River; they feel at home in this little mud-bottomed, spring-fed pool.

Mr. Cory has built a couple of wooden bathhouses. I go into one of the tiny compartments on the ladies' side to find out whether last year's bathing suit will conceal my body, still skinny but considerably taller than the summer before this one. I check to make certain that moths have not been at work in any vital places. Balancing on one foot to pull up this one-piece garment, I look down at the green water between the planks and see a couple of little fishes.

To plunge into Shadow Lake on a steamy summer day literally takes my breath away and cools my body to its core, this coolness lasting an hour or two. We spend a lot of Saturday afternoons at Shadow Lake. Stewart walks on his hands on the wooden piers that jut out into the water.

We pose for the big, black box camera held by Stewart's friend, Ed Willis Barnett, a fellow advertising man. Years later, Ed Willis will focus his camera on the cathedrals and châteaux of France; these photographs will win medals; some will hang in New York's Metropolitan Museum and Museum of Modern Art. Although he becomes best known for these pictures, he is also praised for black and white, human-interest scenes. So that's what Ed Willis is doing at this little swimming hole in rural Alabama, aiming his box camera at me and my family in our scratchy, black wool bathing suits.

# *Elizabeth*

Some random gene cursed Elizabeth with a thin, prominent nose. On Teddy's face, this same type nose conveys an impression of power and strength; on Elizabeth, this Dutch nose (as Miss Rose explains it) resembles a parrot's beak. No amount of powder softens this nose; Elizabeth is careful to pose for photographs facing the camera.

A powerful woman—Queen Elizabeth I comes to mind—can get by with a commanding nose, even make it an asset; a rich woman, despite such a nose, will find no lack of suitors. But for Elizabeth—poor, powerless, sexually repressed— that nose is an almost insuperable barrier to romance. Being the ugly duckling in a family of handsome men and beautiful women, Elizabeth relies on her agreeable disposition, her stamina, her capacity for hard work.

*Note Elizabeth's marcelled hair, feather boa, and sensible watch.*

Compared to Louisville, New Orleans, and Kansas City, Birmingham strikes Elizabeth as a hick town. At the end of her long work days, she swims at the YWCA, goes to picture shows, reads books borrowed from Birmingham's only library housed in a small room in City Hall, or—in desperation—listens to telephone conversations on the party line.

By moving his family back South, Mac hopes—among other things—that Elizabeth will find a husband. She does. When I am eleven years old, I watch Elizabeth get married in front of the stone fireplace in Miss Rose's living room, beneath the plaster of Paris lion.

The bridegroom is not one of her beaux from New Orleans.

Not somebody from the social circles of Frankfort where Miss Rose once reigned supreme. Not even a Southerner whose bloodlines could be easily traced. We know little or nothing about Elizabeth's husband: he is a Yankee. In years to come, Elizabeth herself will appear to forget that she was ever, however briefly, married. But Lee Ola and Elizabeth's other friends never forget titillating mysteries:

*What do you suppose happened to Elizabeth's marriage?*

Undoubtedly she found sex distasteful; Miss Rose would have made sure of this. But many women, indeed Miss Rose herself, have this problem. Something more threatening than sex dooms Elizabeth's marriage. Tearfully, she confides in Miss Rose: on their honeymoon to the East, her new spouse took her to meet his family for the first time. She discovers that he has a handicapped brother. (Shades of Miss Rose's infamous expression *fee-de-da-monk!*) Does this mean that Elizabeth herself might bear a handicapped child?

She cannot endure this thought; she worries day and night. She no longer allows

*Elizabeth, hatless, top left, hosts a club meeting.*

her new husband into the marriage bed. A few weeks after the ceremony in front of the fireplace, Elizabeth files for divorce. Divorce! Unprecedented in our family; almost unheard of in Elizabeth's social circle. She returns home, wrestles with the mimeograph and multigraph machines during the day, sleeps alone in her old bedroom. She reclaims her maiden name; she is once again Miss Van der Veer.

*Elizabeth out for a drive with a beau, chaperone in the rumble seat.*

AFTER ELIZABETH'S DIVORCE, Lee Ola, the Kappas, and her friends in the Cauldron Club introduce her to a few middle-aged bachelors who live alone or with their mothers. These men, well-mannered, comfortably well-to-do, fixtures in Birmingham society, escort Elizabeth to occasional events such as a concert at Phillips High School or a play at the Little Theater. Observing them in Miss Rose's living room, even I sense that Elizabeth's beaux—as we hopefully call them—differ in some mysterious respect from Stewart and his male friends such as Hudson Strode and Ed Willis Barnett. I never ask anyone to explain this difference, least of all Elizabeth. She wouldn't know, any more than I, the answer to such a question.

As the evening draws to a close, Elizabeth knows that her escort will offer a friendly handshake or, at most, a brotherly peck on the cheek; at Christmas, a Whitman's Sampler. Her beaux know that Elizabeth neither wants or expects anything more. Their date has had the desired result: Elizabeth has been seen in public with a man; her escort has been seen with a woman.

# *Dorothy*

Dorothy is pretty in a subdued way. Wearing decorous clothing and leaving her hair its natural shade of mousy brown, she keeps her prettiness somewhat concealed. As if she is afraid to be too pretty lest she arouse sexual inclinations in Ted or, God forbid, some other male. Also she does not regard it as ladylike to show off her looks; in this, as on many another matter, she and Miss Rose hold opposing points of view.

Well aware of Ted's fears, Miss Rose's state of constant alarm, Mac's dark moods, Stewart's and Elizabeth's pulp fiction view of the world—my mother often remarks witheringly:

*All Van der Veers think in headlines!*

*Dorothy and Virginia, Daytona Beach.*

TED: I don't believe I ever remember Dorothy being afraid. The night Virginia came, she was the least perturbed person in the whole hospital. Is she simply not troubled in the least about things that keep me right on edge? . . . Or does she merely not even concern herself with anything except that which at the moment confronts her? Anyway, it's a damn good thing she is like she is.

DOROTHY KEEPS HER distance from Birmingham's social set. She has no circle of childhood friends who gather regularly—decade after decade—within the comfortable confines of a sewing club, book club, or garden club. No, she tells her friend, Bernadine, she is not interested in joining the Junior League; she does not want her name proposed for the Nineteenth Century Club. Unlike Bernadine, Dorothy does not ally herself with mildly activist groups like the League of Women

Voters or the American Association of University Women. Unlike Elizabeth, who takes up with other Kappa Kappa Gamma alumnae, Dorothy has no sorority sisters. She does not play bridge. In truth, my mother only feels really comfortable with the handful of women of her age adventurous enough to have attended Smith, Vassar, or Wellesley. They are kindred spirits; also they are of her class.

Her taste in furnishings and décor reflects her privileged rearing: an antique Oriental rug, suitably worn, and a baby grand piano, gifts from her grandmother but strange sights in such a tiny house; watercolors by the Louisiana artist A. J. Drysdale, a fashionable wedding present in 1920; prints by the Japanese artist Kawase Hasui, acquired after she studied art history at Wellesley; a little pencil sketch of me by a local theater director, Bernard Szold, who has titled it *Infanta Virginia*; a small silhouette of her father bearing the notation: *executée au Sommet de la Tour Eiffel.*

*Dorothy in her best voile; Virginia in organdy with puffed sleeves.*

In small but crucial ways, our surroundings differ from those of many of our neighbors. No concrete fawns, pink flamingos, or wrought-iron loveseats on our lawn; certainly not any white-washed tires with flowers planted inside. Our yardman, Essie, could easily harvest a cedar Christmas tree right in our own backyard. But Dorothy insists, no matter the cost, upon a bought tree, a spruce. One spring, I admire a lush, flowering tree in a neighbor's yard.

*No, Virginia, we don't grow mimosas.*

Mimosas, I take it, must be common.

Dorothy has internalized not only a strong sense of class but also the prejudice of New Orleans grandees against latecomers who arrived on the last boat or live in what is spoken of as *back a' town* or the *Irish Channel.* The wife of one of Ted's Sunday afternoon baseball friends displays a patronizing air because we do not live over the mountain; when the players and their wives have gone home, my mother confides condescendingly:

*Mrs. So 'n so is Irish!*

Dorothy remains reclusive in part because she is shy. But the main reason that she does not involve herself in community or clubs is so she will be ready at all times to do whatever Ted wants, knowing that he depends on her totally.

# Other Voices

And always in our kitchens and backyards, other voices, murmuring, laughing. Making their special noises, the clickety-clack of the lawn-mower, the chomp of axe against oak, the clang of iron lids against a stove, all part of the hum and rhythm of our households.

Miss Rose and Dorothy have been reared to consider four components as essential to life: food, clothing, shelter, and help. During their brief stays in Enid and Kansas City, neither ever felt comfortable with white women in the kitchen. As Miss Rose put it:

*White help won't do!*

(Anyone who does not suit Miss Rose becomes the butt of this expression: So-and-so won't do!)

We speak of our help as servants; by that, we mean colored people. Miss Rose, brought up under the pervasive influence of Stephen Foster's lyrics, occasionally slips up: darkeys. Dorothy retains some of the expressions peculiar to her New Orleans upbringing: *touch of the tarbrush* (What does that mean, Uvvy? Never mind, Virginia!), *octoroon, quadroon.* (I don't even ask the meaning of those strange words.)

Our cooks and yardmen address adult family members as Miss Rose, Miss Dorothy, Mr. Ted; they call me Virginia. Dorothy and Miss Rose address their help by first names: Emma, Mamie, Audrey, Delia, Essie.

Whoever currently holds the job of cook on Exeter Drive or Ridge Road enters the kitchen around 6 A.M., except on Sundays, bangs stove lids and heavy iron pots, starts bacon or ham sizzling in a skillet, and begins to mix biscuit dough. At Miss Rose's house, the first task of a cook—summer as well as winter—is to coax a large, wood-burning iron stove to attain a desired temperature. It is vital that the cook get stewing, frying, and baking out of the way as early in the day as possible. In July and August, temperatures in the kitchen often soar well above 100 degrees. A wooden icebox stands on an adjoining porch, somewhat removed from this inferno.

Miss Rose engages in an almost constant search for help, always hoping to find a husband and wife to live on the place so that the cook will be on hand early to prepare breakfast. Then to make beds, pass the laundry through the wringers, iron shirts and dresses for two men and two women, scrub floors, run the carpet sweeper, tidy up the kitchen. Take a short nap before returning to stoke up the fire and cook dinner. Meantime, her husband is busy stoking the furnace, cleaning the fireplaces, mowing the big yard. Small wonder there's such a frequent turnover. One cook, getting ready to quit, offers a novel excuse:

*I can't live up here in this grove.*

(When things get tense around Miss Rose's place, Elizabeth or Stewart, hoping to make everybody laugh, will repeat that line.)

If Miss Rose has to endure two or three days without a cook, she takes to her bed.

AT OUR HOUSE, the help is more stable. Essie is the only yardman we ever have. Audrey, an untutored girl from the country when she comes to work at sixteen, stays for years. Dorothy teaches her a trade: how to keep house.

Audrey's regular tasks: polish flat silver, also sterling silver vase initialed DRV, silver candlesticks, little silver bell, silver dresser set, also monogrammed; silver serving dishes; polish brass andirons, brass Seth Thomas clock. Everything must shine.

Starch the white, hand-crocheted table mats. Stretch them on the nails of wooden frames until they dry stiff as boards.

Wash clothes, sheets, towels in the washing machine, then pass them through wooden wringers until they emerge barely damp. Hang everything on lines in the backyard on clear days. (Underwear and nighties on the middle line.)

Iron. Put a little starch in Mr. Ted's seersucker summer suits (known as wash suits) and white cotton shirts. Press everything, even sheets, with heavy, new electric iron.

Cook breakfast. Cook dinner. Wash and dry dishes and pots. (By hand, of course).

Dust, vacuum, sweep.

At the onset of summer, put coarse white osnaburg slipcovers over sofas and upholstered chairs to make the house seem cooler. Dorothy purchases osnaburg at the cotton mill run by our friends, the Pickards, who live in a big, white-columned house with their own swimming pool (practically unheard of in Alabama in the 1930s) high above the little mill village of Cordova. The Pickards tell us that osnaburg is the cheapest fabric produced in their mill; weavers even toss lunch scraps into this cloth.

All summer I examine those slipcovers, looking for a tiny piece of lunch meat, a bit of apple peel.

SUMMER: ESSIE'S REGULAR tasks: Wrap the heavy Oriental rugs in newspaper with mothballs inside, tie with strings, drag upstairs to the attic. Bring down the grass rugs, hose them, lay them in the sun to dry, place on living room floor. Mow the big yard with a hand mower. Water the grass, the flowers.

Fall: Prepare flower beds, plant jonquil bulbs, rake and burn tons of leaves, toss grass seed over our big yard so that it will be bright green in winter.

Winter: Chop down trees. Cut them up for firewood. Clean the big coal stove and the fireplaces, take out ashes, lay new fires.

Spring: Check to see if the homemade, wooden picnic table is stable and the benches steady enough to handle twelve people; drape a rope in the trees to hold the fragile, paper Japanese lanterns that, with lighted candles inside, will glow like little pale moons over our outdoor evening gatherings. Pull up the crabgrass. Weed the flower garden.

Essie walks to work from Zion City, a colored community, about five miles each way. He is in our yard before 7 A.M. when Father leaves for work. Essie and Father are the same height; Father is thin as a young pine, Essie sturdy as a full-grown oak.

Dorothy picks up Audrey at the end of the carline; Audrey gets out of the back door of the yellow streetcar and into the back seat of our car. No one instructs her to do this; if Audrey questions this custom, she never lets on to us. Apparently it never occurs to Dorothy—Wellesley notwithstanding—that she is taking part in a demeaning ritual. When they arrive at *Topside*, Audrey enters through the kitchen door.

Every so often, Dorothy announces:

*I'm going to Pizitz today, Audrey, to get you some new uniforms. What color would you like? White? Grey? Black?*

*Two white ones, Miss Dorothy. And this time, I think two blue ones would be nice.*

Essie provides his own overalls.

By tradition, Thursday is maid's day off; otherwise Audrey is on hand five days a week. At the end of work on Saturday, Ted hands out the going rate of weekly pay, Audrey $3; Essie, $4.

Audrey and Essie are Dorothy's daytime companions, often the only people, outside of Father and me, that she sees unless she goes to the grocery store. This relationship has a code of behavior, unwritten but understood by both races: Dorothy and Audrey sit at the kitchen table companionably to shell pecans or to string beans. But not to eat lunch together. Audrey fixes our daily meals but she and Dorothy seldom, if ever, shake hands. Audrey cleans our toilet but she and Essie use the toilet in the servant's quarters back of the garage. Dorothy and Essie never sit down together; never shake hands. Ted and Essie shake hands at Christmas time.

Although the so-called Scottsboro Cases become an international cause célèbre, Ted and Dorothy do not discuss with Audrey and Essie the plight of nine young Negroes hastily convicted of raping two white female vagrants aboard a freight train crossing northern Alabama; rape is not a subject that Dorothy discusses with anyone, even her husband; Ted and Essie speak only about trees, grass, and our supply of firewood.

The back door. The back seat of the car. The uniforms. The first names. Miss Dorothy, Mr. Ted. Yes ma'am. Yes suh. And yet if they resent the indignities heaped upon them—and surely they do—Audrey and Essie do not hold Miss Dorothy and Mr. Ted responsible. All depend upon one another, all behave according to the code.

# *Food, Wonderful Food!*

From shortly after dawn until nightfall, fragrances of food—bacon, ham, onion, garlic, or a cake rising in the oven—pervade our houses, heralding meals to come. Eating is our preeminent sensual experience, openly permissible, and, without a doubt, more frequent than sex.

To reach a downtown restaurant from our remote location requires an almost twenty-mile round trip. On special occasions, we gather around a table at Hooper's Café, attended by a colored waiter in white jacket and white gloves. On lesser occasions, we propel our trays past the cheap and mundane offerings of the Britling Cafeteria while its female organist pumps out "On the Trail of the Lonesome Pine." But, for us, even dinner at the Britling is a rare event.

Consequently, it falls to Miss Rose and Dorothy to oversee, in their respective households, seven sizable breakfasts every week, seven evening meals, Saturday lunch, and a major midday meal on Sunday. Unless we are invited to a meal at the home of friends, there is no escaping this inexorable routine.

Nothing in their carefree girlhoods as Belle of the Bluegrass in Kentucky or Priestess from the South on Tree Day at Wellesley prepared Miss Rose or Dorothy to keep house. Accustomed to ample household staffs, they are particularly ignorant on matters relating to the all-important realm of the kitchen. Granted, neither actually cooks sixteen meals every week. But Miss Rose orders groceries, Dorothy gathers food. Both plan menus, instruct their cooks, and prepare special dishes.

Their kitchens resound with the clang and clatter of stove lids, iron pots, steel bowls, and tin pans as the cooks, Miss Rose and Dorothy, dutifully follow the draconian instructions on their recipe cards, most foods requiring brute strength to prepare:

Beat steadily for 30 minutes.

Stir constantly.

Mash through a colander.

Pat firmly.

Crack the peach seeds.

Grind the almonds.

Pull the candy until it turns.

AS IN OTHER matters of the flesh, Miss Rose has little or no zest for eating. Perhaps her natural inclinations in this regard had been squeezed out of her by the tight corsets and whalebone stays of her youth. Perhaps, as the superintendent's daughter, she confronted too many tasteless meals in the dining room of the Feeble-Minded Institute.

Or perhaps eating might make her (perish the thought!) fat. With this frightening possibility in mind, Miss Rose merely picks at her food, remaining throughout her life as thin and delicate of frame as in her palmy days as a belle. Entering her fourth decade at this repetitious task, Miss Rose constantly grumbles:

*I'm so bored with food!*

Her mind, she protests, is more attuned to Krishnamurti, her time better spent writing letters to Herbert Hoover.

Because her husband, son, and daughter drive the family car downtown each weekday, Miss Rose summons the raw material for her meals by telephone:

*Hello, Sanders and Johnson? Do you have some nice, fresh beets today?*

Later in the morning, Sanders and Johnson delivers the beets and her other needs to Miss Rose's back door. No money changes hands; Mac settles his grocery bill at the end of each week.

Ahead of her time as to food—as in other matters—Miss Rose inclines toward vegetarianism. Although an occasional roast appears on her table, she leans heavily for her main dish on croquettes:

Chicken croquettes.

Salmon croquettes.

Ham croquettes.

A typical Sunday midday dinner at her house consists of chicken croquettes, corn fritters, cauliflower with cheese sauce, Waldorf salad, and angel food cake.

Miss Rose, however, is not totally without her culinary achievements. Whenever I arrive at her house—and as soon as she has stopped fluttering her hands and telling me how worried she has been whether I would get there safely—she ensconces me on her stiff horsehair sofa and proposes:

*Now. How about a nice tea cake?*

With her own hands, Miss Rose concocts tea cakes from flour, sugar, shortening, eggs, milk, and vanilla. Thin, crisp to the verge of dryness, only faintly sweet, tea cakes do not compare in my standard of values with the succulent, chocolaty richness of a Mr. Goodbar or a Baby Ruth. But the name lends them a certain cachet; these are no mere cookies, they are tea cakes.

Miss Rose's other specialty is beaten biscuits (emphasis on the adjective). Other than its name, a beaten biscuit bears little resemblance to ordinary, pliable biscuits, being closer kin to the hardtack consumed by sailors on long voyages. Creating these dry, brittle biscuits, my grandmother mixes flour, water, and lard, beats this dough 500 strokes (*210, 211, 212—don't interrupt me, Virginia, I'll lose count!, 213*), then passes it seven or eight times (until the dough pops) through a series of rollers, resembling a small, hand-operated clothes wringer, then cuts tiny biscuits about the size of doughnut holes.

To offer, at a tea, wedding reception, garden club meeting, or bridal shower, an array of beaten biscuits—cut in halves, brushed with butter, filled with tiny slices of ham, warmed in the oven, displayed on a paper doily—can be counted upon to elicit an admiring chorus of oohs and ahhs.

Miss Rose serves her beaten biscuits in one particular silver compote. With the doily removed, one can plainly see, based on the numerous dents in this vessel, that sterling silver, like dental filling or normal teeth, is no match for a beaten biscuit. (In Miss Rose's era, many another Southern lady made beaten biscuits. But these specialists died off; their descendants, absorbed in mornings of tennis or the selling of real estate, discarded the little wooden rollers and allowed the art of making beaten biscuits to pass into oblivion.)

BEING YOUNG AND new to this responsibility, Dorothy appears to address without complaint the task of feeding a husband, child, and the numerous guests Father brings to our table, often spur of the moment. Perhaps she considers the presentation of exceptional food an essential element of her role. Undoubtedly she needs something to do, her only companions on this remote hilltop being a child, Audrey, and Essie. But, I suspect, the main reason my mother spends so many hours in her hot kitchen is that Father, especially after he gives up his three-pack-a-day habit of Picayune cigarettes, takes great delight in eating.

Having a car available during the week (Father travels to and from work by streetcar), Dorothy fetches the food for her household. This daily trip to the end of the carline comprises her main social outing. The little business district that everybody calls the Loop consists of a barber shop whose proprietor, badly burned during the Great War, treats his ruined face with rubbing alcohol (his customers associate their haircuts with the smell of rubbing alcohol); a shoe shop where Father, Stewart, and Mac get their old shoes resoled; a little restaurant run by a white-haired woman called Miss Daisy; and Hill's Grocery Store.

En route to the Loop, we make our first stop at the Red Rock Filling Station.

*Five gallons of Woco-Pep please, Mr. Epps.*

*Yes ma'am, Miz Vandiver, that'll be one dollar. Hurry back!*

(Father finds this Alabama-style farewell highly amusing; he is tempted to drive around the block and return.)

Then a few blocks to Hill's Grocery Store.

*Good mornin', Miz Vandiver, what'll it be today?*

*I need a can of Calumet baking powder, Mr. Hendrix.*

Mr. Hendrix walks to the baking powder section and brings Calumet, a staple on Dorothy's list, to the counter.

*A jar of Karo Syrup, Red Label, please.*

A short walk to the Karo section and back.

*A five-pound bag of Swan's Down Cake Flour, please.*

If my mother has fifteen items on her list, Mr. Hendrix makes fifteen separate trips back and forth to various counters. Grocerying is a leisurely, structured ritual. During this ceremony, Mr. Hendrix and my mother, aware that they occupy different rungs on the social ladder, chat about the weather or say how awful it is that the Lindbergh baby has been kidnapped, or remark on the amazing birth of the Dionne quintuplets.

After Mr. Hendrix carefully deposits the brown paper sacks in our car (there is no thought of tipping Mr. Hendrix!), my mother and I stop by the icehouse. With a twenty-five-pound chunk of ice wrapped in a croker sack and tied to the running board, we head for home, a dripping trail in the dust marking our passage.

AT DOROTHY'S HOUSE, the art of food preparation reaches a higher plane than at Miss Rose's. Although she never actually cooked during her privileged youth, Dorothy instructs many a reluctant cook in the preparation of pungent New Orleans dishes:

Red beans simmered for several hours with garlic, celery, onion, bay leaf, and parsley.

Grillades, thin rounds of veal, cooked in a heavy pan with green pepper, basil, thyme, onion, and cayenne.

Shrimp coated in the Creole manner with a roux of flour and shallots, then combined with tomato paste and green pepper.

Invariably all those dishes are accompanied by rice. Not gummy brown rice. White rice, each grain blossomed into a light, fluffy, separate existence. Until the end of her long life, Dorothy—brushing aside the advice of nutritionists—remains stubbornly loyal to white rice.

During her girlhood, banana vendors hawked their wares up and down Calhoun Street:

*Banans! Nice, ripe banans!*

This sales pitch made a deep impression on my mother; she prefers bananas that are ripe to the verge of rottenness, skins heavily freckled with brown spots. She teaches her cooks to bake bananas in the New Orleans fashion, covered with a thick syrup of sugar, butter, cinnamon, and lemon, and—after the end of Prohibition—flavored with rum. The aromatic result appears not as dessert but as a side dish to accompany our main course.

Once in a rare while, perhaps for Sunday breakfast, my mother persuades Father to forgo his favorite fried eggs and bacon in favor of *pain perdu* (lost bread), slices of bread soaked in eggs, sugar, nutmeg, and cornstarch, fried in butter, and served with powdered sugar. But generally speaking, Audrey fries eggs in bacon or ham grease, making certain that my father's eggs emerge as flat as pancakes, their yolks firm and dry. If entirely satisfied in this regard, Father coats his eggs with catsup.

Her cooks, in turn, teach Dorothy to fix foods the Alabama way:

Succotash—corn and lima beans cooked with bacon grease and green pepper.

Cornbread (white not yellow).

Grits, either soupy or yesterday's cold slabs fried in bacon grease.

Fried green tomatoes.

Baked hen with cornbread dressing.

Pieces of chicken dipped in buttermilk, then fried in bacon grease.

Stringy, tough country ham cooked at least five hours.

Green beans simmered for hours with ham hock or a slab of fatback.

Baked sweet potatoes topped with marshmallows.

Corn grated from the cob, combined with green pepper, eggs, and milk to form a pudding, then baked until set.

Spoonbread made with grits.

Although he learns to love corn pudding and fried green tomatoes, Father balks at some Alabama favorites, pork barbecue in particular, and, in any guise, okra.

Dorothy also learns a lot about cooking, not from cookbooks but from what she considers a much more reliable source—friends and neighbors. She packs her small wooden recipe box with cards, carefully copied in her cramped, idiosyncratic handwriting:

Bernadine's peach jam

Mrs. Austin's crab

Fannie Belle's punch (serves 25 or 30)

Miss Minnie's meatloaf

Jessie's rum cream pie

Charlotte's cheesecake

Mrs. Smith's pralines

Etc., etc.

WITHOUT EXCEPTION, DESSERT climaxes our evening meals and Sunday dinners.

Soft strawberries over sweet, friable shortcake, the whole mound covered with whipped cream.

Half a juicy cantaloupe with a large scoop of vanilla ice cream melting inside.

Chocolate blancmange lined with lady fingers.

On birthdays and other occasions, a bought cake from Waite's Delicatessen, perhaps an eight-layer concoction, each layer iced with chocolate, the top covered with white icing. Or a coconut cake, so moist that a slice crumbles to pieces before I can get it to my mouth. Or a spice cake thickly studded with raisins.

No use driving downtown and back just to pick up a cake, Father rationalizes. So he and I perch on high stools and watch Robert Waite concoct Father's favorite—double chocolate sodas. Robert puts thick, dark syrup in the bottom of a large, cone-shaped glass, adds two scoops of chocolate ice cream, a few squirts of soda water, and tops off our sodas with big dollops of whipped cream. When Father has assured himself that the sodas are not what he considers watery and that he has the larger serving of ice cream, we set about consuming our treat, slurping noisily on paper straws to pull up the very last drop.

(Secretly I would have preferred one of Robert's chocolate sundaes: a small paper box filled with vanilla ice cream, topped with hot, thick chocolate sauce, and sprinkled with salted almonds. But better go along with Father when he's in the mood for a soda.)

Our meals never end with fruit and cheese. Father being thin to the point of gauntness, Dorothy, young and slender, I tall and gangly, we never skip rich, satisfying desserts nor consider these dishes sinful. We also consume, without a moment's hesitation or a thought to the contrary, eggs, salt, bacon fat, lard, whipping cream. The words calorie and cholesterol are simply not part of our vocabulary. But, at mealtimes, I am frequently the target of a popular admonition:

*Eat everything on your plate, Virginia. Remember the starving Armenians!*

Just exactly how the starving Armenians will benefit if I eat everything on my plate is never made clear.

DOROTHY GOES ALL out for company. If she has a few days' notice, she spends one entire day preparing meringue shells, an airy, delicate concoction of egg whites, sugar, and almond extract.

These egg whites must be beaten—by hand—until frothy. Then more beating, adding almond and sugar until stiff and shiny. This combination put in a pastry bag and painstakingly squeezed into a series of little circular nests. Bake until dry (but not brown!), cool in the oven, store in a dry place until ready to serve. Finally, fill with homemade ice cream—vanilla or, my favorite, peppermint—top with thick chocolate sauce, and present to her admiring guests.

As Christmas nears, candymaking occupies hours and hours of Dorothy's life:

Brittle New Orleans pralines, so sweet that even I can consume only a few at a sitting.

DOROTHY'S DIVINITY
FUDGE
　3½ cups of sugar
　1 cup water
　¾ cup Karo syrup (Red
Label)
　2 egg whites
　Cook sugar, water and
Karo syrup until spins
thread. Remove one cup
and beat with egg whites.
Let the rest cook until
pops in water. Combine.
Spread on marble slab to
cool and harden.

Dark, creamy chocolate fudge.

White divinity fudge, studded with pecans.

But Dorothy attains the apex of candymaking by mastering a Kentucky recipe known as cream candy. Family lore has it that Mac's sister, Aunt Minnie, originated this confection in her Frankfort kitchen and taught the art of making cream candy to other young Kentucky matrons.

Creating cream candy is even more demanding than creating meringues. Dorothy forms a mixture of whipping cream, sugar, and vanilla into a long, heavy rope, pulls that rope for perhaps twenty minutes until she feels in her fingers that it is ready to be laid out on a marble slab. When it dries to the desired consistency—firm yet flaky—she cuts the rope into small pieces.

Ah, cream candy! It literally melts in my mouth.

All, or almost all of this homemade candy (my consumption being usually limited to misshapen pieces or crumbs), is wrapped in wax paper and carefully arranged in tin boxes as gifts. Does Dorothy work at candymaking hour upon hour, day after day, because she has so little else to do? Does she, who sets such store on being proper, consider this a proper gift because it is made by her own hands? Or does she indulge in this annual orgy of candymaking because, even if she must buy a few, new tin boxes, this is a welcome present that she can afford to give. The raw materials—sugar, cream, vanilla, chocolate, pecans—are cheap. The only other ingredients—her time and energy—cost, so she must figure, nothing.

Drink (Alcoholic): Following the demise of Prohibition, Auntie's daughter, Cud'n Mary Yandell Rodman—visiting from Philadelphia for a month—introduces her rustic Southern relatives to a certain Eastern ritual. At Mary Yandell's insistence, Stewart puts down some hard-earned dollars to purchase gin, vermouth, and a jar of green olives.

Miss Rose, a surreptitious sipper from the longest-lasting wine bottle known to womankind (left over from Christmas, she insists), Mac, and Ted remain constrained by Puritanism. I am too young to participate. But to the joy of Elizabeth, Stewart, Dorothy, and their friends, Cud-n Mary Yandell (bless her frosty, Main Line soul!) gets us hooked on that golden moment: The Cocktail Hour. Mary

Yandell goes home. But The Cocktail Hour remains.

THANKSGIVING DINNER: OUR family always eats Thanksgiving dinner at home. Either at Miss Rose's place or Teddy's place. If Dorothy is the hostess, her best white cutwork cloth adorns the table. At the head rests a stack of yellowing dinner plates, veined with fine scratches, each bearing the likeness of a turkey with a majestic ruff. Dorothy inherited a dozen of these antique plates; this year she has set only seven places, there being no visiting relatives from New Orleans or Kentucky. Each place setting is marked by a crystal goblet, fragile as an eggshell. If no one is watching, I tap my goblet ever so gently; it rings like a delicate bell.

Dorothy has set her table, as she does every day of the week, with silver knives, forks, and spoons, the handles elaborately embossed with curlicues, bunches of grapes, and cherubs. On each of Dorothy's first twelve birthdays, her grandmother had given her a complete place setting of this ornate Victorian flat silver, including a large serving spoon and a tiny spoon for stirring the demitasse. Opening this same present year after year, Dorothy must have gotten a pretty good idea of what was expected of her in life.

When I was nine or ten, I used to amuse myself—and annoy my mother—by whispering to guests to look on the back of their spoons or forks. Obeying my great-grandmother's instructions, the jeweler at Coleman E. Adler & Sons in New Orleans inscribed each piece with the date of that particular birthday. Whoever had a piece of silver dated 1898 had part of the oldest place setting. And knew my mother's age. But there is no use playing this mischievous game with only the immediate family present; everybody around the table knows how old Dorothy is.

Our group begins to assemble. At the very last minute, Stewart makes his entrance, walking on his hands. He teeters thus for a few seconds before righting himself, red-faced and triumphant.

The women shriek:

*Stew-art!*

I giggle and join the admiring chorus:

*Uncle!*

Father, still thin as a scarecrow, seats himself at the head of the table. Because it is Thanksgiving, he is happy and cheerful; with his family around him, he feels safe and secure. Miss Rose, in her best white dress, sits at Teddy's right. Elizabeth opposite. Stewart and Mac on either side of Dorothy. I between Elizabeth and Stewart. The men's places are distinguished from those of the women by small crystal ashtrays.

My mother, who orchestrated this dinner, tinkles her little silver bell, heralding the cook's grand entrance. In comes Audrey, mindful that, at this very moment a few years back, the Lancaster china platter that matches the turkey plates had broken in half, splattering the big bird and its contents onto the Oriental rug. Although Dorothy glued the halves together, she has prudently instructed Audrey to undergird this platter with a tin tray. Thus protected, the turkey arrives safely in front of Father, his big silver carving knife and serving fork at the ready.

Our family is not in the habit of asking a Higher Power to bless our food. To hold hands around the table would be unthinkable; we do not go in for public expressions of physical attachment. (Or private ones either, for that matter.)

The omission of this rite is Father's decision. Eternally puzzled as to the meaning of human life, Father has no intention of calling upon a deity of whose existence he is not entirely certain. Given a choice between possible heresy and certain hypocrisy, he takes the chance of being considered a heretic because he deems hypocrisy by far the greater sin.

I am taking it all in. Stewart's clowning. Elizabeth's meekness. Mac's weariness. Miss Rose's futile attempts to turn back the clock. My mother's propriety. My father's uncompromising purity in thought and deed.

Father carves. Audrey passes the plates. When all seven have been served, Dorothy lifts her fork. Without further ado, we begin our meal.

# Virginia

Thank heaven, I do not have the Van der Veer nose. But for one so young, I have a number of imperfections; most obvious, a jagged scar on my right cheek. As a two-year-old in New York City, I fell and cut myself. Dorothy, at twenty-three, knew nothing about cuts; she didn't even know the name of a doctor. Even if she had, perhaps we would not have had the money to pay him. So she simply closed my gaping wound with a piece of sticking plaster. By the time she took this bandage off (ugh, what a shock that must have been!), it was too late for stitches. I was permanently scarred. (Eighty years later, this scar is still visible.)

Both of my knees are scarred; the aftermaths of falling in an effort to catch a pop fly on the softball diamond at *Topside*, to steal home during a kickball game at school, and other strenuous endeavors. Stewart loves to call attention to my knees:

*Those knees.*

*Virginia has knees like a livery stable horse!*

My left arm is decidedly smaller than my right arm and slightly crooked. Before I reach my twelfth birthday, I break this arm during a kickball game at school; I break it skating down the only paved sidewalk within ten miles of home; I break it by simply falling down a steep bank. Consequently, I spend weeks of my childhood with my arm bent at the elbow, encased in a stiff plaster cast held up by a cotton sling.

When I break my arm the second and third times, I weep and wail; my arm will be back in a cast for the next month. Even worse, I know by now that I have brought Uvvy and Father to the brink of financial catastrophe: the doctor's bill will be a staggering one hundred dollars!

*Virginia, with Wolf Solent.*

To top off my flaws, I have two small teeth on either side of my front teeth; my little teeth have never been capped, perhaps for the same reason that the scar on my face was never stitched. Before I arrive at public school, I never gave a thought to my irregular teeth; once I make my appearance at Robinson Elementary, my schoolmates can't seem to get enough of this subject:

*Virginia, I just love your cute, little baby teeth!*

THERE BEING NO other children on Ridge Road, my Saturday playmate is eighty-year-old Miss Mame, the mother of our neighbor, Mrs. Thomas. Confined to a wheelchair, Miss Mame has little entertainment other than to listen to the radio and to play Parcheesi with me.

Mr. and Mrs. Thomas are ahead of their day. In the 1920s, few, if any, older couples leave the Midwest to seek a warmer climate; they just live and die in Ohio. Furthermore, Mr. Thomas enjoys a strange new status: he is retired. My grandfather goes downtown to work every day; Mr. Thomas putters around his house, fixing things. In earlier life, he was an engineer. I question Uvvy:

*If Mr. Thomas doesn't work, where do they get money?*

She does not know the answer.

The Thomases have another distinction: they are the only Christian Scientists we have ever known. Unlike fickle Miss Rose, the Thomases are second-generation Christian Scientists. In the Thomases' world, no one ever dies; they pass on. Miss Rose is quick to adopt this new, optimistic parlance. Mr. and Mrs. Thomas are also fond of sayings such as Mind over Matter and Hold the Thought. I put it to Uvvy:

*If mind is over matter, why is Miss Mame in a wheelchair?*

ANOTHER RETIRED COUPLE moves onto our hilltop; this notion of retirement must be catching on. In different ways, Mr. and Mrs. Austin are as exotic as the Thomases. Mrs. Austin, a formidable woman with an imposing bosom, invites

my parents to call her by her nickname; out of her presence, we practice saying
it with a straight face: Dodo.

Mr. Austin lived through the great San Francisco earthquake of 1906; he never
tires of telling this story. On Saturday nights, Mr. Austin goes downtown to the
Municipal Auditorium to watch wrestling matches. Nobody else we know goes
to the wrestling matches; Uvvy disapproves:

*Of all the common things!*

The Austins employ what they refer to as a manservant instead of a woman
cook. Cleveland lives on the place. One day when Essie is clearing crabgrass off
the baseball diamond and I am practicing with my bow and arrow, strong whiffs
of cologne waft over our front yard. We cannot see the source because a steep
bank hides Ridge Road, but we know it is Cleveland, headed for the Loop on his
day off to catch the streetcar to town.

Essie mutters, as if to himself:

*Some nigger's gonna kill that loud-smelling Cleveland someday!*

I convey this information to Uvvy:

*Essie says some colored man is going to kill Cleveland because he wears so much
perfume. Why would somebody do that?*

*Go on over to the Thomases, Virginia, and play Parcheesi with Miss Mame.*

NEW NEIGHBORS RENT a house about a block away in city terms. Jim Rivers
claims that he actually makes a living as a writer, spinning what he calls railroad
"yarns," fabricating short stories that bring in a few checks, and aspring to write
a novel. His wife, Ethel, types the final drafts.

One quiet, summer day after the Riverses have lived on our hilltop almost a
year, Uvvy, Audrey, Essie, and I hear a piercing scream. Ethel calls:

*Help! Help!*

As the grownups rush to her aid, Uvvy orders:

*Go straight to Miss Mame's, Virginia.*

We have high drama in our family: Teddy's nervous breakdown, Daddy Mac's
depression, Elizabeth's flight from marriage, Stewart's occasional rebellions against
his father. But no one ever screams out loud.

Later I learn—mostly from Audrey and Essie—that Jim Rivers, despairing over
his lack of success as a writer, locked himself in the bathroom and slit his wrists.
Essie broke down the door. Ethel, Dorothy, and Audrey managed to staunch the

bleeding. After the crisis subsides, Ethel insists that they move away from the scene of her husband's attempted suicide. They pack their sparse possessions and board the train back East.

A few years later, Father gets a jubilant letter from Jim. His first novel, a mystery, is to be published by Doubleday Doran. His agent hopes to get it serialized in some important monthly.

I DO NOT play with dolls; I consider them dull. Actually I possess only one doll, Hitty, with a prim china face and a long, Puritan costume. For Christmas, I have made it clear that I prefer books. For everyday companionship, I depend on Inky, our faithful Scottie, and our German Shepherds, Wolf Solent named for the hero of the book by John Cowper Powys, and Joseph Conrad, named for the author of Father's favorite novel, Lord Jim.

*Virginia, in aviator cap, waiting for the mailman.*

Wolf Solent and I sit on one of the stone pillars that guard our driveway, waiting for the mailman. We will be able to hear the motor, stopping and starting, a half-mile away, no other car being likely to traverse Ridge Road this entire afternoon. I am wearing my favorite headgear, a leather aviator's cap with goggles and ear flaps, like the caps worn by two of my heroes, Charles Lindbergh and Amelia Earhart.

I hope the mailman will deliver a little, white cardboard box with my name on it. I am forever writing off for free samples. Weeks pass. Finally the samples straggle, one by one, into our mailbox; a tiny tube of Colgate's toothpaste, a little jar of Pond's hand cream; a small bottle of Jergen's lotion smelling like almonds. And—my dearest wish and secret sin—a miniature Tangee lipstick.

It is imperative that I bring in the mail; if Father spots that Tangee lipstick, he will forbid me even to dab it on my lips in the privacy of the bathroom. Or worse, he will confiscate it.

Wolf pricks up his ears. Now I, too, hear the scratchy sound of a motor. The mailman is coming! Oh, I hope it's lipstick day!

# The Playing Fields

Thump! Wooden bat meets fat softball. Onlookers roar home run! Yeah! Where are we? Ebbets Field? Shibe Park? Fenway? Yankee Stadium? Birmingham's Rickwood Field? No, this rowdy softball game is going on in the side yard of our house at *Topside*; Ted has sacrificed enough trees to make a softball field. Not regulation size, but this diamond serves his purpose.

Almost every Sunday afternoon during mild weather, Father summons couples from the city to make up teams for his little park. Bold visitors take turns at bat, tending base, or in the field: Charles Zukoski, Jr., trust officer of the First National Bank; newspaper columnist John Temple Graves II; pianist Dorsey Whittington (thereby putting his long fingers at considerable risk). Of course Father is the star; years later, a neighbor remembered his boyhood awe:

*Mr. Van der Veer hit the ball a country mile!*

Less agile men—*Birmingham News* editor James E. Chappell, stockbroker Mervyn Sterne, and Alex Wellman (an actuary who has figured that the odds on this bumpy turf overwhelmingly favor broken bones)—remain prudently on the sidelines with the wives.

Our former neighbor, Jim Rivers, in a letter from his new home in the East, describes our Sunday afternoon gatherings in the prose of a seasoned author of pulp fiction:

> We're wondering if D. Whittington might have pitched a six-hit shutout against somebody or other. Or whether V. Van der Veer lined out to John Temple [Graves] at Third with the bases full in the last half of the ninth. *(Indeed I did not!).* And we're wondering if the screened porch looks as

it always did, touched with the inviting charm of a place made for rest and relaxation. And whether you sat later in the still darkness, under the lordly trees, and talked softly of yesterday and tomorrow while distantly the dotted belt of lights marked the restless city.

*Virginia on the homemade tennis court.*

BEYOND THE BASEBALL field, we build a tennis court, tennis being Dorothy's favorite sport. A simple matter really. Get Essie to cut down some trees. Mark off a flat space (regulation size, this time). Order several truckloads of Alabama red clay (cheap as dirt). Enclose this space with wire. Set two iron posts in concrete, purchase a rope net. Lo, the tennis court!

Of course, that's not the whole story. Before we can play, Father or Essie must fill a heavy metal roller with water from the garden hose, then roll the hard-baked clay as smooth as possible. I fill a little wheel with powdered lime and propel it over the court to mark off fresh lines (*Virginia, don't let it wobble!*). All players pull weeds.

Only after all those procedures do we unscrew the presses from our wood racquets. If feeling unusually spendthrift, open a new can of fluffy white balls. Air rushes out: whoosh!

Growing up near Audubon Park in New Orleans, Dorothy taught herself to play tennis. Now she teaches her husband (who swings his racquet like a baseball bat) and her daughter. Because I cannot beat her, I storm off the court, weeping. Tears don't move Uvvy; she refuses to give away a single point:

*Be patient, Virginia, your day will come.*

My parents even consider having Essie dig a swimming pool. After all, we live in Roebuck Springs. Father hires a dowser to search for water with a forked piece of willow called a witch wand. If the witch wand bends toward the ground, chances are there's water beneath. But the willow does not even twitch. Miss Rose can't resist an I-told-you-so:

*Now, Teddy, if you had built down in the valley like I wanted you to . . .*

WE HEAR OF a new, faster sport requiring a court smaller and easier to build than the tennis court. In less than a day, Essie clears ground for the badminton court.

Guests who think they are merely invited for dinner—an aesthete like Stuart Mims, for example, whose primary interest is choosing next season's soloists for the Birmingham Music Club—find themselves, light racquets in hand, attempting to chase down a little airborne object. Father explains patiently:

*Now Stuart, hit the rubber end, not the feathers!*

Other nonathletes like Mervyn Sterne, who simply will not play baseball, tennis, or badminton can invent no excuse to avoid what appears to be a dignified and leisurely stroll on the lawn. But our rural brand of croquet is fierce:

*Knock the ball into the woods, Mervyn. Better yet, into the road so it will roll down the hill.*

One summer Ted instructs Essie to dig two pits far enough apart for tossing horseshoes. But we don't take to horseshoes. Too common a sport, I suspect, for Dorothy's taste. Mysteriously and without prior notice, the horseshoe pits are filled up; that space becomes an archery range. When there's nobody around to play tennis, Uvvy being busy making Christmas candy, I take out my steel bow and send wooden arrows whanging in the general direction of the bull's eye.

When I turn eleven, Uvvy comes up with a novel idea. Perhaps to put me in the company of other children, she enrolls me in a class on tap dancing.

Our teacher calls the movements:

*Left foot: Tap 1, 2, 3, Hop!*

*Right foot: Tap 1, 2, 3, Hop!*

Then a more complex set of commands:

*Left foot, then right foot: Tap 1, 2, 3, 4, 5, 6, 7.*

It is quickly apparent to all concerned that I have no future as a tap dancer.

*Winter sport on a homemade sled.*

As a boy, Ted had been marbles cochampion of Frankfort, Kentucky. His rival, he tells me, was a colored boy; their final match ended in a draw. He clears a circle of red clay:

*Hold it like this, Virginia, against your knuckle.*

But I can't muster any enthusiasm; marbles is Father's game.

When it rains, we hold Ping-Pong contests on Miss Rose's big side porch, and Elizabeth revels in her rare chance to shine.

Birmingham's country club set having moved over the mountain, the Roebuck Country Club, with its golf course and simple wooden clubhouse surrounding a spring-fed pool, is now open to the public. (No use bothering to add new-fangled chlorine: this water is cold enough to freeze any germ!) But even for natural athletes like Father and me—born to play almost any sport—golf is an alien realm. It never occurs to us to pay for lessons; we simply haul off and swing, Father wielding his driver like a baseball bat.

Since we swim in Shadow Lake or Roebuck Club pool, ride Stewart's horses, possess a veritable arsenal of baseball bats, tennis and badminton racquets, Ping-Pong paddles, croquet mallets, a bow, a target, arrows, balls of all sizes and shapes, badminton birds, horseshoes (briefly), marbles called puries, aggies, smokies, and allies, plus playing fields for all those sports right at our front door, who needs golf? Who needs a country club?

*Virginia, astride Stewart's (safely tethered) Arabian.*

IF WE CANNOT round up enough players to form two softball teams or to comprise a rowdy cheering section for croquet, Uvvy, Father, and I simply head out the door for a walk. Ore miners and bootleggers have made rough trails through the dense woods back of our house. Occasionally a couple of men appear out of this seemingly uninhabited forest. From a safe distance, they give us the once-over. Could this tall stranger be using a woman and a child as cover in order to sniff out their illegal moonshine stills? They decide not. As quickly and silently as they crossed our path, the bootleggers vanish.

The ridge back of *Topside* is a spur of Red Mountain, the great ore range of the South. We follow the miners' rough roads until we reach the mouth of a mine. Not a soul around. The mine, like hundreds of others, is closed, a casualty of the Great Depression.

*Please, Father, let's go in!*

Absolutely not. Father knows that miners will refuse to go back into a mine if they learn that a female has even set foot inside—a bad luck omen.

# *Private School*

Around 7:30 A.M., unless it is raining or snowing, I walk down our steep hill, carrying my lunch box and books, amble about a half mile on Valley Road, turn onto a little byway, and enter the back gate of the John Frye property. Along the way, I am joined by Mary Glass who lives at the foot of our hill; Kitty Sims and her little brother, Ezra G. (whom we call Junior); and Harry Horner. At the gate, we meet up with Leroy McDavid and Ikey Strange who have walked from the other direction.

All of us, ten at most, are headed for school in a former carriage house behind the Fryes' big house. This school exists for one purpose only: to provide companionship for the Fryes' son, Roland, until he is old enough to go East to prep school. Mrs. Frye (whom Roland calls *Mater*) has rounded up a few neighborhood children and hired a teacher, Mrs. Tarrant. No one bothers about standards, tests, or accreditation; no one would think of raising such matters with the indomitable Mrs. Frye. If she wants to have a school in her backyard, that's nobody's business but hers.

Consequently, Mrs. Tarrant assigns her pupils to whatever grade she chooses; if she has three fifth graders and only one child ready for the fourth grade, she simply promotes that one child:

*Now Virginia, you go on into the fifth grade.*

It is rumored in our neighborhood that Roland's father (whom he calls *Pater*) is a millionaire. The Fryes are of Scottish descent and inclination: it is reported that Mr. Frye, on pleasant days, walks the seven miles to work at the First National Bank to save a nickel carfare.

Certainly Roland's material possessions are out of the ordinary: he has his own shoot-the-chute, a wooden roller coaster on which we coast down his sloping

113

*Disgruntled May Queen, at far left; Roland is King.*

yard propelled by gravity; he has a private lake and a lawn so big that our kickball field occupies only one small corner. His family has a uniformed chauffeur to drive their big Packard with its cunning little fold-down seat in the rear.

Roland possesses armies of lead soldiers attired in the uniforms and battle gear of many a war. On rainy days after school, Roland and I play war: in particular, The War Between the States. Roland always outmaneuvers me; if he is their leader, even the troops in gray win.

Mrs. Tarrant chooses me over Mary Glass to be Queen of the May (of course there is no question who will be the King). Mary is a little older and a lot more sophisticated than I but my flaxen hair gives me the edge: who ever heard of a brunette May Queen?

But my head is not turned by wearing a crown and a long white dress and standing next to King Roland. Indeed I enjoy it much better when I am cast the following year as the jester in our school play. I love my homemade jester costume of many colors. Uvvy has adorned it, even the cap, with little bells that tinkle when I move. For months after the play has ended, I don my jester outfit and run around our yard, bells tinkling.

Other than its name, I like everything about The Roland Frye Private School. I like playing with Roland's lead soldiers and riding his shoot-the-chute. I like kickball; I try so hard to steal home that I break my arm running into Ikey, who is dead set on stopping me. (And succeeds.)

But when my report card filled with A's arrives in the mail, I complain: Uvvy, why does the report card bear the title, The Roland Frye Private School? Ask Mrs. Tarrant, Uvvy says. But no use bothering Mrs. Tarrant; she has her hands full teaching pupils in five different grades. Also, she knows which side her bread is buttered on.

*Mrs. Tarrant (in hat) and her entire student body: top row, from left, Virginia, Kitty Sims, Mary Glass, Roland (seated); Ezra Sims, front row, second from right; others unidentified.*

(Many years later, when I travel in the Scottish Highlands, tales about the crofters and the laird strike a faintly familiar chord. What does this relationship remind me of? Oh yes, now I remember. )

To celebrate the end of the school year, all ten of us go to Avondale Park and gaze at the park's lonely elephant, Miss Fancy. After that picnic, Uvvy breaks the stunning news: next fall I am to enter eighth grade in a public school. It is time, my mother decrees, for me to leave the cloister of Roebuck Springs and experience the real world. This coming fall I am to observe my eleventh birthday.

# *Sunday School*

Once in a while, Father gives up his dreary Sunday morning symphonies and announces that we are to attend the Independent Presbyterian Church. This is one of those Sundays; it's been five months since we last made such a pilgrimage.

I dread sitting beside a grandmother who wears white in winter and exercises her eyes during the sermon; even worse, I dread going to Sunday School with children who attend virtually every Sunday. I cannot seem to get the hang of Musical Chairs. I suspect the regulars of having a secret signaling system. Otherwise why am I, a natural athlete, always left standing when the music stops?

I particularly hope that Mrs. McIntosh, a handsome soprano noted locally for her spirited rendition of "Hanging Apples on the Lilac Tree," will not be in charge of Sunday School today. But she is. She spots me immediately—the little lost soul who comes so seldom. At one point during the morning, she inquires sweetly:

*Virginia, do you know the Lord's Prayer?*

*Yes.*

*Good, dear.* (Pause) *Recite it.*

With everybody listening, I cannot, for the life of me, get through the Lord's Prayer unaided. My classmates snicker.

Further interrogation from Mrs. McIntosh:

*Now, dear, where were you baptized?*

If the truth be known—and I devoutly hope that the truth will not be known in front of the entire Sunday School—I have never been baptized. Dorothy and Ted do not believe in dictating religion to a mere child; I am to be allowed to make up my own mind about this matter when I grow up. But I fudge:

*I don't remember.*

*You don't remember?*

But my mortification over Musical Chairs, the Lord's Prayer, and the subject of my baptism pales in comparison to my singularity upon attending Sunday School on Easter. Surrounded by little girls in pale pink, blue, purple, green, or yellow organdy dresses with straw bonnets to match, white patent leather Mary Janes, little white gloves, I am wearing my regular Sunday dress.

Uvvy explains:

*Now Virginia, only common people parade around in new dresses at Easter.*

When the service ends, Uvvy, Father, Miss Rose, Elizabeth, and I make a beeline for home; there is to be a softball game on our little diamond this Sunday, maybe that will get my mind off wishing I had been born common.

# *Just Look at All Those Books!*

Our rural neighbors possess little in the way of reading matter except a copy of the Bible and perhaps a current edition of *The Old Farmer's Almanac*. Upon entering our living room, they appear awestruck at the sight of Father's shelves. Hoisting his small daughter to his shoulders, one visitor commands, as if indicating a wonder on the scale of the Grand Canyon:

*Just look at all those books!*

Struggling to understand—and to recover from his personal collapse—Father immerses himself in the works of numerous philosophers, mystics, and theologians, among them Reinhold Niebuhr, Paul Tillich, Thomas Merton, Albert Schweitzer, Rabindranath Tagore, Thomas à Kempis, Rudolf Karl Bultmann, Thomas Kepler, Evelyn Underhill, C. S. Lewis, Søren Aabye Kierkegaard, Marcus Aurelius, C. P. Snow, Arnold Toynbee.

Mr. Smitherman, our longtime plumber, after a day spent repairing our pipes and listening to Father hold forth on esoteric topics, reports wonderingly to his wife:

*Mr. Van der Veer is readin' and studyin' about a world we don't know nothin' of.*

While at Tulane, Teddy became acquainted with the high-minded, main character of Joseph Conrad's *Lord Jim* and the tortured protagonists of Edith Wharton's *Ethan Frome* and Somerset Maugham's *Of Human Bondage*, thereby displaying early on what was to become a lifelong proclivity for accounts of inner turmoil, moral dilemma, spiritualism, mysticism, and the occult. He explored these topics with a fellow student, Stringfellow Barr. "Winkie" Barr, as Teddy knew him, was to complete his education at the University of Virginia and become in

1936 president of St. John's College in Annapolis, Maryland, where he would implant a classical curriculum (still in effect), grounded in the "great books" of Western Civilization.

When Teddy married, his fellow editors and reporters on the *New Orleans Item* presented the young couple with a twenty-five-volume set of the writings of Mark Twain. In their typeset message, his colleagues expressed high hopes for Teddy, then a crusading reporter bent on the never-ending task of "cleaning up" the French Quarter. These small, green books, along with *Lord Jim*, a two-volume first edition of H. G. Wells's *The Outline of History* that sold a record two million copies after its publication in 1920, a leather-bound set of the *Collected Works of Robert Louis Stevenson*, and Tolstoy's *War and Peace*, are presences on our shelves, almost members of the family.

When Father takes refuge in raw, sooty Birmingham, its streets laid out barely fifty years earlier, a city known for rampant anti-Catholicism, religious fundamentalism, and as home to the South's largest klavern of the Ku Klux Klan, what possibility could there be for a life of the mind? To his surprise, he quickly discovers, in the person of M. B. V. Gottlieb, a Russian emigré and proprietor of one of Birmingham's three bookstores, an urbane and knowledgeable bibliophile. Thereafter almost every book we acquire bears an inconspicuous label: The Studio Book Shop, 409 N. 20th Street, Main 7903.

On the inside covers, Gottie, as friends call him, carefully pencils the price: for example, $1.75 for F. Scott Fitzgerald's *This Side of Paradise*; a surprising $3.50 for *A Book About Myself*, Theodore Dreiser's autobiographical account of his newspaper days; and, after the great crash of 1929, $1.00 for Charles Morgan's *Portrait in a Mirror* and $1.50 for Sinclair Lewis's *Dodsworth*.

On Christmas, birthdays, and other occasions, Gottie can be counted on to add his personal contributions to the stack of books we always receive. For Christmas, 1926, he gives my parents a boxed three-volume set of *The Diary of Samuel Pepys*, bearing in his tiny handwriting the message:

*My good friends, Ted and Dorothy, I come to you by Pepys!*

I, too, benefit from Gottie's literary taste and generosity. Like Father, who read these worn editions in his childhood, I also grew up on romanticized depictions of post-Civil War Kentucky (Annie Fellows-Johnston's *The Little Colonel*) and of our family's ancestral homeland (Mary Mapes Dodge's *Hans Brinker or the Silver Skates: A Story of Life in Holland*).

Gottie sets in to elevate my literary taste. No more doings of the Bobbsey Twins, Jack and Jill, Diddie, Dumps and Tot, or Miss Minerva. No more adventures of Tarzan or the Hardy Boys. I am old enough, Gottie insists, to move beyond favorites such as *Little Women, Little Men, Jo's Boys, Tom Sawyer, Huckleberry Finn, Hitty: Her First 100 Years,* and *Peter Pan.*

VIRGINIA, January 17, 1931: I went to Roland's and played until 12 o'clock. I have $3.20 in bank. I had a fire in my room and I finished *Ivanhoe.* It is the best book I have read yet.

(I am ten years old.)

During long, dull summers, I consume a book a day from the East Lake Public Library, reading my way through its entire children's department by age eleven; then using Uvvy's card, starting in on the adult department, including much of Dickens and Edward Bulwer-Lytton's *The Last Days of Pompeii.*

As Christmas nears, Gottie steers my relatives firmly in the direction of chronicles that widen my world, such as A. Conan Doyle's *The White Company,* Charles Dickens's *Oliver Twist,* Thomas Hardy's *The Return of the Native,* Plutarch's *Lives,* and William Makepeace Thackeray's *Henry Esmond.* If I must have adventure, he suggests—to my great delight—James Fenimore Cooper's *The Deerslayer* and *The Last of the Mohicans.*

At Father's instigation, Gottie, then a bachelor, builds a dacha near us. One cold, winter night, a fire on our remote hilltop reduces that wooden house to rubble, destroying not only valuable icons and paintings brought from what he calls the Old Country, but also Gottie's cherished collection of rare first editions.

For weeks after that fire, I poke around in the ashes of Gottie's dacha. But the fire fed voraciously on the paint and enamel of Gottie's treasures; I cannot find a trace of his carved wooden toys and spoons, his wooden boxes bearing images of fairy tales, folklore, and animals, or his *matryoshkas,* big, wooden dolls, hand-painted, with nine or ten smaller dolls nested inside, each holding a different animal or flower. Not even a drop of amber survived that fire; not even a chip of Gottie's blue and white Dzhil china.

When I finish the first year of high school, Gottie presents me with a leather-bound copy of James M. Barrie's *The Little Minister* and this gentle reminder:

> To my great friend Virginia because you and I remember the first book you read, I am sending you this one J. Barrie at the end of your first journey so to speak through bookland and knowledge-land. Luck speed you on! And may you never lose that first asset, your love of reading.

(Thank you, Gottie. I never did.)

FATHER'S EARLY PURCHASES at Gottie's bookstore are obviously inspired by his own brief experience in the Great War. Romanticizing his stint in the Navy, Father is attracted to the works of writers who, like H. M. Tomlinson, simply love the sea. However he much prefers authors who had worked at sea but whose writings deal with moral exploration and tests of character as, for example, the works of Knut Hamsun, the Norwegian one-time fisherman whose *Growth of the Soil* won the 1920 Nobel Prize, and Conrad, whose *Victory* joins *Lord Jim* on our shelves.

*"Our nightly pleasure"— Virginia (opposite page) and Teddy.*

Father also evinces an early partiality for the work of women writers such as the English novelist May Sinclair, with her taste for Freudian psychology; Matthew Arnold's niece, Mary Augusta Arnold, who apparently felt obliged to sign her novels by her married name, Mrs. Humphry Ward; Vera Brittain, who wisely chose a pen name rather than that of Mrs. George Edward Gordon Catlin; and Ellen Glasgow, whose *Barren Ground*, an unflinching account of poor-white Southerners, must have been a bracing tonic for my father, reared on *The Little Colonel* and John Fox Jr.'s *The Little Shepherd of Kingdom Come* and *The Trail of the Lonesome Pine*.

Alerted by Gottie, Father knows when authors come to town by train to promote their books. Long before the advent of talk shows, writers who bother to include Alabama on their tours have few duties other than to meet the book editor of the local newspaper and sign a few autographs at The Studio Book Shop.

With little warning to my mother, Father chugs up the hill in his Locomobile, proud to show our modest home to some stranger from afar—usually England. On October 19, 1926, one visitor writes in Father's copy of *Fortitude*: "To Mc-Clellan Van der Veer with the best wishes of A. Hugh Walpole who has been happy this evening."

In 1930, another dinner guest inscribes *The Meaning of Culture* "To Ted Van der Veer. John Cowper Powys." Attending Cowper Powys's lecture at Phillips High School, Father had been delighted to hear this sentiment:

> The only chance for realizing happiness, contentment or whatever term it may be called, is in living the simple life. A little house, a garden, and good books should meet the needs of any man.

But he may have been a bit disappointed in Cowper Powys's terse inscription. Not only has Dorothy treated this author to a rare, home-cooked meal but Ted has introduced him to our dog, a German Shepherd named Wolf Solent for the hero of what Cowper Powys considers his finest novel.

TOURING BRITS BEING few and far between, Father usually has to content himself with the companionship of local writers. Growing up in a neighborhood where writing is virtually a cottage industry, having an aunt and uncle who retreat to their "claw-sets" every night trying to become writers, and with a spinner of railroad yarns, Jim Rivers, living right next door, I naturally assume that every family contains writers.

The most widely known writer of our acquaintance, Hudson Strode, upon capturing our neighborhood belle, Theresa Cory, moves her to Tuscaloosa. Still Theresa keeps in touch with her old neighbors, giving Elizabeth a headache and setting off strange vibes at our dinner table.

Another young woman in our neighborhood, Rose Smith, marries John Temple Graves II who pontificates each morning in his column prominently displayed (along with his photograph) on the front page of the *Birmingham Age-Herald*. Dorothy and Ted become good friends with Rose and John but their paths are to diverge in the late 1930s, the Graveses becoming more conventional by living over the mountain and Graves beginning his shift from ardent admirer to truculent critic of President Franklin Roosevelt.

Besides Elizabeth, there is another woman writer in our neighborhood, albeit a secret one. Not even her closest friends know that stately, dignified Mrs. Ross Cullon Smith—Rose Graves's mother—does anything in life other than preside over a beautiful house and garden. Who would ever guess—we did not—that Miss Jessie is the author of an occasional philosophical column on the editorial page of the *Birmingham News*, headed "The Wanderer" and ostensibly written by a man named Lewis Follett. But there is no Lewis Follett. Like many another married woman of privileged station, Mrs. Smith is taking no chance that gossips might jump to the shameful conclusion—totally erroneous—that Ross Smith's wife has to work to help support their family.

It is public knowledge, however, that Mrs. Smith holds the key to a private chapel built by her family, pioneer settlers of the area around these springs. Young women of our neighborhood, Theresa Cory for example, have only to ask; Mrs. Smith is happy to let them get married in Wilson Chapel. She gives a key to the back door of her chapel to James Saxon Childers, a Rhodes Scholar and English professor at Birmingham-Southern College. Childers writes in this studio.

In one of his newspaper columns, Childers recalls the day that a man on a large black horse rode up to his windows and introduced himself:

> Ted had to stoop as he came into the chapel for he is three or four inches over six feet . . . he just rode over to welcome me to Roebuck and to ask if there is anything he could do for me. "Such as lending you a horse," he said.

Two days later, they take a long horseback ride. Jimmy (as we call him) on Dixie, Ted riding Gypsy, followed by his dog named Joseph Conrad. Childers is invited to dinner; the two talk long into the night about God, philosophers, and poets.

In 1925, Childers edits a limited edition of the tales of Mother Goose, published in London with hand-colored illustrations and Chinese cover paper. He writes travel books and unsuccessful novels, the most venturesome being *In the Deep South: A Novel About a White Man and a Black Man*. This story of the barriers to friendship between male Southerners of different races sinks almost without a trace, probably because in 1936 this is a topic ahead of its time and because Childers (in contrast to Lillian Smith's later sensation, *Strange Fruit*) only hints at the then-ultimate taboo, sexual attraction between men and women of the two races. Through his contacts with these literati, Father meets a fledgling poet, John Beecher, a great-great nephew of the abolitionists Henry Ward Beecher and Harriet Beecher Stowe. John will prove unable to endure the prevailing racial, political, and intellectual climate of Birmingham. Upon departing, he gives my parents a copy of his first book of poems, *Here I Stand*, inscribed:

> *To Dorothy and Ted, upon going away but not from you.*

Eventually John Beecher will grow a white, Whitmanesque beard and attract a following as a poet who, like his famous ancestors, champions the cause of racial justice.

IF HIS WRITER friends become caught up in their own projects, Father presses more conventional friends, like a banker, a stockbroker, an insurance actuary, and their wives, to spend long evenings at our house, reading aloud. Through my bedroom walls, I am lulled by the murmur of Father's voice reading William Alexander Percy's ode to white Southern planters, *Lanterns on the Levee*. In 1934, our thin walls vibrate with expressions of shock and injured pride when the group reads *Stars Fell on Alabama*, a forthright representation of Alabama in the thirties by a Yankee observer, Carl Carmer.

Other than these and the books of Thomas Wolfe, Father evinces little interest in the contemporary Southern novel. Works by William Faulkner, T. S. Stribling, and James Agee are conspicuously absent from his collection. Maybe—living in Birmingham—my father has his fill of the burdens and peculiarities of his poor-white neighbors. Furthermore, he does not read Margaret Mitchell's *Gone With the Wind*, his ancestors having fought for the Union and his ideal of womanhood being my genteel mother, not feisty Scarlett.

Perhaps due to the lingering influence of Prohibition, Father conceives the notion that to read a play aloud would be a law-abiding and elevating way to observe New Year's Eve. Everyone must have a part, thereby insuring that all celebrants stay awake. Father's group rings in 1935 by reading the French playwright Jacques Deval's comedy *Tovaritch*; in later years, he is to mandate more serious fare such as *Hamlet*.

Father's favorite literary figures—for example, Hamlet and Joseph Conrad's Jim and Axel Heyst—reflect his own dilemma: they, too, are high-minded men of honor and conscience, struggling to find their place in an immoral world.

# PART FOUR

# The Great Depression—
# The 1930s

# A Family Business

ac still stands beside Miss Rose, still handsome. Even Dorothy, who has married their beautiful son, says that her father-in-law is the handsomest man she ever laid eyes on.

But now Mac wears a shabby suit, a black felt hat to hide his baldness, an air of defeat. He has suffered one crushing loss after another; his young father, his career at Labrot & Graham, his daughter Eleanor, most of his life's savings in the Enid venture. The father who preaches strict business ethics to Stewart and Teddy, who tries so earnestly to hearten his sons in their times of doubt and fear; the grandfather who grins as he holds me in one hand high above his head, who hugs me as we pose on the steps at Miss Rose's place, has become a bitter, old man who retreats into sullen silence or erupts in anger over a mere kettle of fish.

Of all Mac's choices—New Orleans, Enid, Kansas City—none has led to failure so deep, so long-lasting, as his decision to start a mail advertising business in Birmingham shortly before the onset of the Great Depression. The Magic City: what a cruel joke! Of its 108,000 wage earners, 25,000 will soon have no work at all; most of the rest will work part-time. Only 8,000 will earn what they did before the stock market crash of 1929.

> VIRGINIA: Poor Daddy. He went to Montgomery today to try to get a job in the whiskey business but was rejected because of his age. It's hard to get old.

Of all the nonessentials in this stricken city, sending little leaflets through the mail must rank near the very top. What business can afford to advertise? What

customers can afford to buy? The Van der Veer Company is virtually bankrupt; its partners cling together for dear life.

ELIZABETH, February 8, 1933: . . . February is a week old and we have done $25 worth of business to date. We have all sat around because it's hard to get down to anything when things are like that. I read a few books but in those straight chairs and being worried, it's not much pleasure. Had lunch with Lee Ola . . . she came back to the office and stayed about an hour, talking. We're in the midst of winter's worst weather, the thermometer being 19. Some snow today.

March 4, Inauguration Day

February—without par the dullest month in Van der Veer [Company] history. Total business for month about $160 . . . days when I

*A family business: the Van der Veer Company, ca. 1930. Top, from left, Ted, Mac, Elizabeth, Stewart. Middle, the women wear smocks to protect their dresses. Right, a day in the office.*

did nothing but sit by the stove and crochet or read. More than a week went by without an order.

March 1st was the most exciting day . . . All morning long there were rumors of the banks closing. About two o'clock it happened—an extra told of Governor Miller's closing the banks for a ten-day holiday (later changed to Friday with the privilege of drawing out 5%).

Dad had seen it coming and drawn out $35. This we divided between the 4 of us [Mac, Stewart, Ted, Elizabeth] and Bert [employee], so now everybody has the clothes on his or her back, a few dollars, a little gas and that's all . . . I had $4 of the spoils—gave $2 to Mama and still (4 days later) have $1.80. I spend a nickel or dime on lunch . . . the bank closing didn't get the [Van der Veer] Company for much because we were out of money anyway.

I was wondering where I was going to get the money to pay the $25 or $30 I owe, when, lo and behold, there now is a moratorium on all debts . . .

The Kappas had tea at Mrs. Lanier's and then dinner at Waggoner's (everyone regretting to part with their sixty-five cents, very precious now.)

We let the cook go and also Bert, so we are down to bedrock . . . And what a day for Franklin Delano Roosevelt to step into the picture as president! Heard his very fine speech over radio.

March 8:

10¢ lunches, one fire in the office stoves, no cook in the kitchen. I still have a dollar of the 4 given me a week ago . . . We took in $12 worth of work today . . . so tired and worried sometimes that I don't care what I look like—hair flying wild and face dirty. We sent the cow up the road . . . let Richard [handyman] go.

March 22:

The banks opened peacefully and calmly after Roosevelt made a quieting talk over the radio . . . so that's that . . . Bessie the cook has left.

By April, the Red Cross Family Service, which aided 510 Jefferson County families in April 1927, struggles to deal with a caseload swollen to 23,077 families. By June, the Federal Emergency Relief Administration reports that 22.7 percent

*Elizabeth, a bad day at work?*

of all Alabama families—almost one-fourth of the state's population—are on government relief rolls. We are not on relief—but we're close.

Our family has enough to eat; how that happens I do not know. Unless our grocery money comes from the small check my mother receives each month from her grandmother's estate. We don't waste a bite; if I leave my piece of bread too long in the open-faced toaster, Uvvy orders:

*Scrape off the burnt part, Virginia. The inside is perfectly good.*

Same thing with the two ends of the loaf:

*Turn them the other way around, Virginia, spread the peanut butter on the inside, no one will know the difference.*

However, I know the difference; tough end pieces don't taste as good as soft center slices. But at least I don't hear any more talk about those starving Armenians.

Even though we have no money for shopping, we can still afford the nickel fare for a streetcar ride to town and back. We window shop on Third Avenue; Uvvy is wearing her frayed brown coat. I lag a step or two behind, hoping no one will think that I am with her. I am going on twelve, an age to be easily embarrassed by my mother's old coat.

Timidly we venture into Burger-Phillips. In the best of times, we never got off the elevator on the Third Floor (Better Dresses); now we cannot afford the Budget Dresses on the Fourth Floor. But it doesn't cost anything to look.

Elizabeth is the mainstay of the Van der Veer Company. Stewart and Ted pick up and deliver on foot; they try to bring in new orders. Mac keeps the books when he's of a mind to do so.

But Elizabeth knows how to operate the mimeograph and multigraph machines that turn out those little advertising flyers. Her hands are always stained blue or black; she wears little rubber thimbles in an unsuccessful effort to spare wear and tear on her broken fingernails. She pushes Bert Hendrix, the printer, and her assistant, Mary Sudderth, to meet deadlines. She worries constantly. No wonder Elizabeth suffers from what she calls blue periods and nervous exhaustion. She thinks she cannot go to the doctor until she finishes paying (on time payments) what she owes from her last visit. She tries to cure her ailments by staying in bed on Sundays.

> ELIZABETH: Have finally located the cause of trouble on the jobs. Stencils were dried out. Am relieved to know it was nothing we had done.
>
> If jobs are late, they're late! I've gotten to the point where I can't worry anymore.
>
> Worked until 1:30 (Saturday). So tired I went to bed at 9 o'clock. Everyone singing the Music Goes Down and Around.
>
> A mean DeBardeleben [coal company] order kept me from going to club meeting, also from accepting an invitation to lunch at the Country Club with Lee Ola.
>
> A $70 account closed its doors today.
>
> More trouble with the job. It's driving me nuts. I'm as nervous as one of the Dionne quintuplets. If I could have a couple of weeks vacation but not a chance. Finances too critical.

BUT ELIZABETH DOES manage to get a couple of vacations—free. The *Birmingham Post* sponsors a contest:

> Why It's Smart to Read The Post and Why It Pays to Shop the Ads
>
> Just write 50 words or less. Be sure to include a sales slip, theater stub, or a purchase memorandum from a *Post* advertiser.

Those who compose the most eloquent testimonials win all-expense trips to Pensacola, Florida, five hours from Birmingham by Greyhound Bus; six nights in the San Carlos Hotel, and meals.

Elizabeth does not have to rack her brain

Here they are—the merry Birmingham folks who are enjoying ee vacations at Pensacola as guests of The Post. It was "Come on in, the water's fine" when Gulf coast fun was pled by the vacationists at the Island Casino beach, which with asling white sand, is one of the most famous in Florida. Its at-ons are but one of the many delights offered Birmingham resi-or best answers to the statement "Why it's smart to read The and "Why it pays to shop the ads."

*Elizabeth, left, on her free beach trip.*

for reasons why it's smart to read the *Post*. She serves as hostess, seeing to it that
no one drowns, gets drunk, acts fresh, or otherwise embarrasses the *Post*.

  She even has a couple of dates with a desk clerk at the San Carlos.

In March 1936, Elizabeth secretly observes her thirty-fifth birthday. (Ssh, don't
mention this to Miss Rose!)

  Elizabeth: To be 35 seems no different from any other age.

  But it is. To reach thirty-five in Elizabeth's day is to enter middle age.

# Musicales

In spite of everything, we sing. Except that now there is no soprano to offer "'Tis the Last Rose of Summer," Anna McClelland's beautiful voice having gone down the male line. Stewart, Teddy, and (rarely) Mac offer solos. Elizabeth remains silent. I am willing but squeaky on the high notes. Uvvy minces no words:

*You've no voice, Virginia!*

For once, Miss Rose seems content with a secondary role. In what she calls her music room, she accompanies on the upright Kurtzmann as she learned to do as a student at Ward Seminary in Nashville. If we gather at *Topside*, Dorothy, having practiced Ted's favorites for hours, presides at the keyboard of her Steinway baby grand. Our audience consists of neighbors and friends from town.

Our concerts always begin with opera. Stewart likes rousing songs where he has a chance to spread his arms and furrow his brow. He favors the active, the dramatic, the hackneyed. Actually he is a baritone, like Mac. But if he fancies a particular tenor solo, such as Alfredo's "Drinking Song" from *La Traviata*, he's not above giving it a try.

Stewart begins. To warm up, Escamillo, describing the life of a handsome toreador in "The Toreador Song" from *Carmen*. Then Figaro, bragging on his job as a barber in *The Barber of Seville*:

> *Largo al factotum cella citta.*
> Make way for the town's most useful citizen
> Figaro the barber, Figaro here, Figaro there, Figaro everywhere.

Now, Stewart says, a little something that reminds him of his days as an ambulance driver in Italy, "La donna è mobile" from Verdi's *Rigoletto*. Stewart enjoys translating this ditty:

> Women are weather vanes
> Fickle their choices.

And, now, for his final selection, a tenor solo. This is the clown Canio, playing the role of Pagliaccio in Leoncavallo's Italian opera *Pagliacci*:

> *Vesti la giubba*

*One of Stewart's exuberant handstands, in a different context.*

> *Ri-di, Pagliac-cio*
> Laugh, clown, laugh
> For the love that is dying.

This solo ends with an agonized sob. Stewart relishes this. Concluding his part of the program, he stands on his hands, to great applause.

Teddy, the real tenor, goes in for the dreamy and the plaintive, Rodolfo to Mimi in Puccini's *La Bohème*:

> *Che gelida manina*
> How cold your little hand is
> Let me warm it in my own.

Next Radames's famous solo from Aïda, revealing his secret love for the captive Ethiopian girl:

> *Ce-le-ste Aï-da*
> *For-ma di-vin-a*

Now Teddy offers the peasant Nemorino's tender solo from Donizetti's *L'Elisir d'Amore*:

> *Una furtiva lagrima*
> A furtive tear

Then, from Flotow's *Martha*:

> *Ach so from*
> Like a dream

He ends with his idea of a jolly tune from *The Student Prince*:

> Overhead the moon is beaming
> White as blossoms on the bough
> Nothing is heard but the song of a bird
> Filling all the air with dreaming.

*Mac, in the prime of life.*

PERHAPS MAC, IF he is in a good mood, will join in, just to give the neighbors a taste of the baritone so sought-after in Frankfort at Christmas and at funerals. One song in particular: his all-time favorite, "Avant de quitter ces lieux, Even Bravest Heart May Swell in the Moment of Farewell," from Gounod's *Faust*. Or, for a change, Alfredo's father in *La Traviata*, recalling his son's happy childhood in Provence by the sea:

> *Di Provensa il mar*

Lighter fare follows, from vaudeville or Broadway:

Stewart:
>On the Road to Mandalay
>Where the flying fishes play
>And the dawn comes up like thunder
>Out of China crost the Bay

Or the "Volga Boatman Song":

>Yo, heave ho!

Or "La Golondrina"

Then Teddy and Stewart together, mournfully:
>Oh Danny Boy,
>The pipes, the pipes are calling

Ted alone: "Sylvia"; "Ramona"; "Beautiful Dreamer"; "Annie Laurie"; "Macushla"; "My Heart at Thy Sweet Voice"; "Where'ere You Walk"; "The Hills of Home" (Ted's voice always cracks on the highest note of the word hills); "Believe Me If All Those Endearing Young Charms"; or "Ah, Sweet Mystery of Life!"

All three together, Mac having gotten into the spirit of things, "My Wild Irish Rose" or "I'll Take You Home Again, Kathleen":

>I'll take you home again Kathleen
>Across the ocean wild and wide
>To where your heart has ever been
>Since first you were my bonny bride

>The roses all have left your cheek
>I've watched them fade away and die
>Your voice is sad when e'er you speak
>And tears be-dim your loving eyes

>Oh, I will take you back Kathleen

To where your heart will feel no pain
And when the fields are fresh and green
I'll take you to your home again

(Is Mac singing to Rose?)

By this time of evening, we—the women, the neighbors, the friends from town—are awash in sentimentality, practically in tears. If we are in Miss Rose's music room, she signals the end of the evening by striking up the familiar, the heartrending. All stand:

The sun shines bright on my old Kentucky Home
'Tis summer, the darkies are gay
The corntops ripe and the meadows in the bloom
While the birds make music all the day . . .

The young folks roll on the little cabin floor
All merry, all happy and bright
By'n by hard times come a knocking at the door
Then my old Kentucky Home, good night!

Weep no more, my Lady,
Oh, weep no more today
We will sing one song for my old Kentucky Home
For my old Kentucky Home, far away

The musicale is over. Nothing—not even "The Star Spangled Banner"—follows "My Old Kentucky Home."

IF A SATURDAY afternoon softball game on the diamond at *Topside* is called on account of rain, opera takes its place. Professional opera, that is, broadcast by radio from New York's Metropolitan Opera with unctuous commentary by "The Voice of Opera," Milton Cross. On rare occasions, the Birmingham Music Club brings a touring opera company to town. Father arranges to meet Arturo di Filippi, who is to sing Radames in *Aïda*; with a couple of hours' notice to Dorothy, he brings this Italian tenor home to dinner.

By means of the record player, Ted sets in to educate his long-suffering neighbors as to the glories of opera.

> Virginia: Played *Traviata* at Wellmans' Christmas Eve from 11:30 to 1:30 A.M.

On many a bright Sunday morning, loud peals of doom and despair pour from Father's record player. We are not going to church these mornings; I suspect that this is Father's idea of penance.

Ted is drawn to music that reflects his own hopes and terrors. When Dr. Edmonds's sermon fails to address his needs, or if he derives no comfort from the works of Thomas à Kempis, Marcus Aurelius, Kierkegaard, or his other favorite philosophers, he turns to nineteenth-century romantic composers of music steeped in melancholy and spiritual themes.

So Father subjects us on Sunday mornings to: Richard Strauss, *Death and Transfiguration*; Liszt, *Les Préludes*; Tchaikovsky's *Pathétique Symphony*; Beethoven's *Missa Solemnis*; César Franck's *Symphony in D-Minor* and *Panis Angelicus*; and Wagner's Preludes to *Tristan and Isolde* and *Parsifal*.

When Father puts Sibelius's dark, somber *Fourth Symphony* on the record player, I can stand it no longer. I flee to the now empty servant's quarters in the back of our garage, an old Victrola having been exiled here along with some records of which Father disapproves.

I crank up the Victrola, set the needle carefully at the first note of Nelson Eddy's robust voice singing "Rose Marie" or "Stout-Hearted Men" or "I'm Falling in Love with Someone." Or I dance around this small room, singing along while Rudy Vallee croons:

> Just Molly and Me
> And Baby Makes Three
> How Happy We'll Be
> In My Blue Heaven

My reedy voice, reverberating in the empty servant's room, sounds just fine, thank you, Uvvy!

# *Public School*

First day at Robinson Elementary:

Bailey, Black, Carter, Douglas, Lewis, McDonald, McGill, Owen, Ryan, er . . . er . . . Vandiver? Am I saying that right, Virginia?

My family has never condensed this name, despite the tedium of spelling it for everybody we deal with, sales ladies in particular. Indeed Miss Rose made things worse by insisting—when she bought that coat of arms—upon breaking Mac's birth name, Van Derveer, into three words and changing the capitalization. Coming near the end of the roll-call, my Dutch surname, unlike the easily spelled and pronounced Scottish or Irish surnames of the great majority of my classmates, strikes teacher and class as foreign, even suspect.

Dorothy and Ted chose my first name solely for its alliterative quality. Three Vs and six syllables (or seven on the tongues of purists like New Englanders) seemed sufficient to them; no need to overdo things by adding, for example, Valerie or Vivian. Nor to ruin the whole effect by inserting Sue, Jo, or Anne. But the sound of a single first name breaks the rhythm of a roll-call composed of an almost unbroken string of double names: Martha Belle, Mae Ella, Mary Elizabeth, Jo Ann, John Henry, Bobby Joe, etc.

My teacher asks my middle name. I answer in a whisper: I don't have a middle name.

Classmates snicker.

I might have been less conspicuous had I answered to Ginny, Ginger, or almost any nickname. But I am no one's Sister; my tall frame becludes Bitsy; Miss Rose and Dorothy never inflicted upon me an indignity such as Baby or Boo-Boo. Except in the case of Teddy, our family does not use diminutives. Only her brothers, on their rare visits to *Topside*, presume to call my mother Dot. Adults speak to one another by full names, pronouncing every syllable:

Stew-art. Eliz-a-beth. Dor-o-thy. Vir-gin-ia.

It is my turn to be surprised, when visiting my new schoolmates, to discover that honey, hon, darlin' sweetheart, baby, sugar, or precious adorn almost every sentence. Dorothy, brought up under the stern influence of a father of German descent, does not indulge in sentimental language. I never hear her call my father sweetheart or honey. Of all the adults in either of our households, only one calls me baby or darlin': Audrey.

Adults in our family simply do not use terms of endearment; in this matter, as in sex, we are repressed. If Miss Rose had ever addressed her as honey, Elizabeth, thunderstruck, could only have concluded that her mother had taken up yet another newfangled religion. And as for assuring one another frequently, casually, and publicly that I love you—as will become the fashion later in the century—we are about as likely to utter this endearment as to run through the neighborhood stark naked.

WORSE IS YET to be revealed. This new eighth grader fails to add the customary ma'am or sir following yes or no. Uvvy has specifically instructed me not to say ma'am or sir; only common people, or colored people, she says, use terms so plainly implying inferiority or servitude. When I answer simply yes or no, the class seems to hold its collective breath. But, dearly as I yearn to be like everybody else, ma'am and sir stick in my throat. I try saying Yes, Miss Jones, or No, Mr. Bowie. But this stratagem fails; teachers regard me as disrespectful if not outright mutinous.

Further, my classmates note, I use odd terminology to denote members of my immediate family; these slip out despite my efforts to suppress or alter them. Almost universally, my fellow eighth graders speak of their paternal ancestor as Dad or Daddy; this new girl uses the word Father, a term of address that most of them reserve for the Supreme Being.

In their households, Dad's counterpart is Mom or Momma; mine is Uvvy, an embarrassing holdover from babyhood. Dorothy herself never suggested that I use the simple Mom; surely she would have considered this common. Besides, those words just don't go together: Father and Mom.

Father. Uvvy. Mummy. Daddy. Why is this new girl not satisfied with plain, everyday Mom, Dad, Grandma, Grandpa?

I, AN ONLY child, am surrounded by classmates who can boast of siblings in three, four, even five other grades at Robinson. Not to mention first, second, and first-once-removed cousins. Hordes of aunts, uncles, and in-laws crowd their dining room tables at Thanksgiving; relatives by the hundreds gather annually at simple, country graveyards to clear weeds from the last resting places of their ancestors. (Hard to imagine Miss Rose, her sights fixed on reincarnation, participating in this latter rite.)

FINALLY—MY CLASSMATES NOTE—I have yet another peculiarity. When I get up the courage to speak out loud, I do not sound like them. Immediately they divine:

*You're not from here!*

But the happenstance of being born in Kansas City does not account for my accent. Language is influenced by one's peer group.

Before emerging onto the big stage of Robinson Elementary, I never had what will become known as a peer group. A case could be made that my peer group had consisted of one little girl in New York where I first learned to talk, four native Kentuckians, a mother from New Orleans, my Parcheesi opponent, Miss Mame, from Ohio, Roland Frye with his upper class accent and his use of archaic terms like *Mater* and *Pater*, and Audrey and Essie who retain a lyricism of speech harking back to Africa. No wonder I talk, as my classmates put it, funny.

JEAN AND MILDRED take pity on me:

*We're having a graduation party at our house Friday night. You be sure to come, you hear?*

To my surprise—horror—boys attend the graduation party. We sit awkwardly around the living room, girls on one side, boys on the other, until Jean announces:

*Everybody come out on the porch. We're going to play Spin the Bottle.*

I've never heard of this game. I ask Mildred:

*How do you play Spin the Bottle?*

She giggles:

*Wait and see.* (A boy spins the bottle. When it stops, pointing to a girl, the boy kisses that girl.)

Oh, murder! What would Father think?

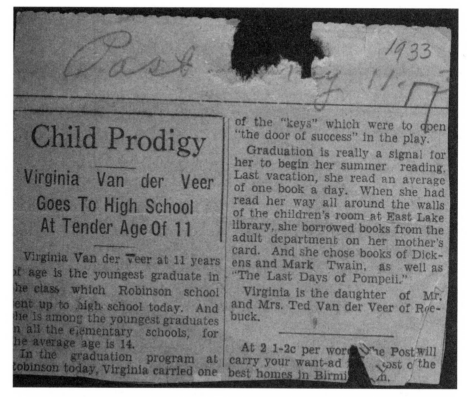

Child Prodigy
Virginia Van der Veer
Goes to High School
At Tender Age of 11

Maybe Mr. Yancey Bowie, the principal, proud to draw attention to Robinson Elementary by claiming the youngest graduate in the entire Birmingham elementary school system, placed that tidbit in the *Birmingham Post* of May 11, 1933.

But I am not a child prodigy. Mrs. Tarrant, with her casual system of promotion at The Roland Frye Private School, has sent me leapfrogging into high school in the company of fourteen-year-olds who understand what Spin the Bottle implies—and Heaven only knows how many other worldly matters.

Now look what you've gone and done, Mrs. Tarrant!

# *Possum Hunting*

Unlike most of our Alabama neighbors, the men in our family do not shoot deer, doves, or quail. Mac and Ted do not hunt at all. Stewart owns no gun; our family does not approve of guns (influence of Miss Rose's pacifism).

Stewart not only lives in a déclassé neighborhood; he engages in a déclassé form of hunting. Possum hunting lost caste when the Southern gentility, aping the British as usual, took up fox hunting. That left possum hunting to poor folks in need of food. After they catch a possum, they fatten it for a few weeks, butcher it as they would a pig, boil it, bake it, and serve it with rich gravy and sweet potatoes.

What would Miss Rose say if Stewart brought a sack of possums to her kitchen? Unimaginable!

One reason Stewart takes up possum hunting is because it's cheap. No fancy red coat, no shiny black boots, no thoroughbred jumper, no bugler. All you need to go possum hunting is a pair of overalls, a shirt rough enough to withstand briers, heavy-soled boots, a couple of twenty-five-dollar hounds, a bull's horn to summon the dogs, and a burlap sack (gunny sack, we call it) to hold the possums.

I start going possum hunting with Stewart when I am about eleven—old enough to be allowed out at night, not old enough to have my thoughts on boys. The season begins about 8 P.M. when nocturnal animals begin to move about. Sometimes we stay out until dawn.

What possesses Father—so beset by fears—to permit his young daughter to stay out all night? Is he not prey to his usual morbid imaginings: I will break a leg, drown in a creek, be bitten by a snake, get lost? It must be Uvvy—who has no fears—who gives me permission to go stumbling through the woods with

Stewart, a couple of his men friends, Elizabeth, and a few country boys who speak respectfully to Mr. Stewart.

Sometimes we are joined by one of Stewart's girls (the term girlfriend being not yet in vogue). The girl may be a clerk in the Purse and Gloves Department of Loveman's, a secretary at Alabama Power, or even a post-debutante eager for a colorful adventure to describe to her married friends.

All of us trail after Jim, a big colored man whom Stewart jokingly calls his Master of Possum Hounds. If there is no moon, the only light in this deep forest comes from the carbide miner's lamp that Jim wears on top of his cap.

Stewart's hounds, Old Bess, Steamboat, and a pup named Bugle Ann, excited and eager, almost drag Jim into the woods. Finally Jim unsnaps the leases. Unlike bird dogs, possum hounds don't rush off; they amble around for a while, sniffing, snuffling. In no time at all, Bugle Ann pipes up. Jim is unmoved; he knows his dogs. The pup, he tells us, is running a cottontail. Bess and Steamboat, too wise and experienced to be taken in by a rabbit, have not emitted a sound.

We wait. Finally a deeper, mellower sound. Jim pronounces:

*That's Steamboat.*

When Steamboat speaks, that means possum. We stand silent, listening to the rhythmic baying as the hounds circle through the woods, closer, then further away, then closer again. Suddenly their tune changes, becoming choppy and frenzied. Jim announces:

*They're lookin' him right in the eye. Let's go, chillun!*

We follow Jim unquestioningly, through blackberry patches studded with briers, branches as big around as Stewart's arm; down into muddy sinkholes, up hills slick with pine needles. Elizabeth and I, being regulars, zip along. Much to our amusement, the girl from town stumbles and falls.

We find the possum clinging with its little black feet and long tail to a limb of a small tree, its mouth open in what looks like a silly grin. In the glare of Jim's lamp, its eyes gleam like diamonds. Jim chains Steamboat and Bugle Ann to a sapling; in their excitement, these hounds might tear their quarry to pieces. Bess will treat the possum more gently.

Jim shins up the tree and begins to shake and jerk the limb. The possum falls to earth with a thud; it tries to fool us by playing dead. Jim plops the first catch of the night into his gunny sack. Off we go, dogs, men, boys, girls, in search of a second possum.

Usually we bag three before Stewart puts his lips to the bull's horn, takes a deep breath, and summons his dogs in for the night. The country boys head for their beds. Jim departs, a sack of possums over his shoulder. The rest of us, muddy, bedraggled, and tired, cook wieners and boil coffee over the fireplace at Stewart's cabin. Privately the city girl vows never to accept another date with this man.

ON MONDAY, STEWART makes his rounds downtown. He boasts:

*Caught three possums Saturday night!*

His acquaintances express amazement. A receptionist at Bell Telephone Company enthuses:

*Oh, Stewart, I wish you'd take me possum hunting sometime.*

Ah, a new audience! Stewart sets the date. He really loves possum hunting—being in the woods at night, listening to the music of the hounds. But even more important, Stewart loves being talked about as a possum hunter. How odd! How romantic!

*Opposite page, Stewart (top left) and Stewart and Ted (bottom photo) and helpers (top right) show off our hunting dogs. Above, the quarry is treed.*

# Writing for the Pulps

I spend a damp, chilly January night at Miss Rose's place, Uvvy and Father being off to a symphony concert. Miss Rose, Mac, Elizabeth, and I huddle close by the big fieldstone fireplace in the living room. In honor of my visit, there is an unusually large pile of red coals in the grate. Elizabeth is working on a contest:

Win $10. $20. Just finish this line in 25 words or less. I like Cashmere Bouquet Soap because . . .

By similar verbal juggling, Stewart recently won two ten-dollar checks from R-ah-C Cola as we call Royal Crown Cola; a neighbor actually won an Electrolux icebox!

Stewart pads downstairs in an old wool bathrobe, a pair of Indian moccasins on his feet:

*How about reading this story out loud? I want to hear how it sounds.*

Miss Rose turns off the radio. Mac lowers the *Birmingham News*. I put aside the exploits of Ivanhoe and the fair Rowena. Elizabeth reluctantly ceases to fiddle with a paste pot and scissors.

Miss Rose announces:

*Six-Gun Gambling Man*

*by Stewart Van der Veer.*

Slight pause.

*Rudy Brant hated himself, cursed himself for a rabbit-hearted coward but he rode steadily westward, luring his piebald gelding through the purpling dust . . . Brant saw a water hole at the trail's edge. He loosed his reins and the pony buried a dry nose in the welcome pool.*

*Whang!*

*A bullet smacked the water, ricocheted among the clump of scrub oaks. A high-pitched voice called across the dusky silence:*

*Set tight, Jud Drury!*

Miss Rose plows gamely on. Mac's face is impassive. Elizabeth smoothes out the soap wrappers that she must send in with each entry. I sneak a peek at Ivanhoe and the fair Rowena. After another thirty minutes, Rudy Brant wins out.

Elizabeth, who has heard this story countless times, feels no need to comment. Mac maintains his usual silence. I say dutifully:

*That was good, Uncle.*

Miss Rose, too, feigns enthusiasm:

*Why Stewart, that was real exciting!*

The literary salon adjourns.

AFTER DINNER ALMOST every evening, Stewart sequesters himself in front of a black Underwood typewriter in his large clothes closet (our family pronounces this *claw-set*), his eyes shielded from the glare of a naked light bulb by a green eyeshade such as those used by copyreaders on newspapers, his toes warmed by the feeble red glow from an open-sided bread toaster.

He is trying to become a short story writer. But Stewart, wisely, does not aspire

*James Saxon Childers profiled Stewart and his writing career in* the News-Age Herald *in 1939.*

*The Loafers at a 1933 Rotary Club luncheon in their honor. Dr. Henry Edmonds, front, second from left; Stewart, front, far right.*

to the *Atlantic Monthly* or *Harper's*. He sets his sights on a group of magazines known, for the spongy quality of the cheap paper on which they are printed, as the pulps. Specifically, Western pulps. Had he not served nine months with Pershing on the Mexican border? Lived six months in Enid, Oklahoma? Who knows the Wild West better?

Although Stewart writes five nights a week for a solid year, he has yet to win a single acceptance. He tries to console himself with the knowledge that Birmingham's most famous writer, Octavus Roy Cohen, wrote 323 stories before coming up with a formula based on the sepia character Florian Slappey whose antics in Birmingham's Negro district are causing white readers nationwide to slap their knees and cackle.

In desperation, Stewart invests fifty dollars—a small fortune—to hire the expertise of a literary agent whose ad he has seen in a trade magazine. This self-styled professor—after cashing Stewart's check—sends the first lesson: submit three plots. Three weeks later, the professor chooses one of Stewart's plots. Now, he instructs his pupil, write the lead—not more than three pages. After several exchanges of letters, his coach okays Stewart's lead. Now write the middle. Rewrite it several times. While Stewart struggles, the professor goes to Hollywood to work, he hints, on a movie script, instructing Stewart:

*Send the ending to my L. A. address.*

For six months, Stewart and his agent ship bits and pieces of the story back and forth across the continent. Finally the professor pronounces "Justice in Rimstock" finished.

Lo and behold, as promised in the ad, the story sells! A check follows: Forty-three dollars!

Adding up the professor's fifty-dollar fee, postage, paper, envelopes, and typewriter ribbons, Stewart is only $10.85 in the red. Not counting his time, two hours a night, twenty nights a month for six months.

Nonetheless Stewart feels rewarded. He can look his friends in the eye; he is to be, at last, a published author. He joins The Loafers, a writing group organized by Octavus Roy Cohen, made up of Dr. Henry Edmonds, three or four local newspapermen, Stewart, and a few other unknowns.

In August 1933, the Birmingham Rotary Club honors The Loafers. A group photograph of Birmingham's distinguished writers appears in the *News*. On the front row—white suit, striped tie, socks to match, modest expression—sits Stewart Van der Veer.

IN THE CLAW-SET of her bedroom, Elizabeth—following, as always, Stewart's lead—also tries to write for the pulps. She, too, struggles to master a formula that will appeal to pulp editors; she, too, chooses a topic about which she knows virtually nothing—love.

*Elizabeth's efforts to sell pulp fiction were also profiled in the local newspapers.*

ELIZABETH: March 6, 1933: Put in about 3 hours yesterday on my current story named This Violet Business. It's rather discouraging to drag oneself to the typewriter each day in the face of existing condition [all banks in the United States are closed] but it just must be done for the sake of discipline [and the hope of some extra money].

March 8, 1933: Am going to try and do 3 pages tonight on my story . . . finish the rewrite tomorrow. Then over the weekend will get Stewart to go over it with me.

March 22, 1933: Am beginning my fourth story of the year—about a Louisiana plantation and as usual am all steamed up about it.

Three years later:

January 20, 1936: *Sweetheart Stories* editor returned story she's had three months. Hell!

January 21, 1936: I am sitting here trying to conjure up a Western romantic plot.

Weds. Feb. 8-1933

Well, here goes for another journal --
seems to me I always pick the ebb tides
to do this sort of thing. However, this
one I will work a little differently,
writing on it each night as I come to
do my work and doing it on the typewriter-
so hoping to make it a little more regular. Also it will help me to get warmed
up to my other work.

Lord, if I thought a year and a half ago
when I started that other journal thinking it marked a low point, but I didn't
know nothing. That was a boom compared
to this A.D. Feb. 8- in the years of the
depression (for it seems to be everlasting)
and three weeks prior to Roosevelt's inauguration. February is a week old now
and we have done $25 worth of business to
date. For a week now we have all sat
around and I mean sat around, too, because
it's hard to get down to anything when
things are like that. I read a few books,
but in those straight chairs and being
worried, it's not much pleasure.

I told Bert today I was going to bring
down a radio, my crocheting and a rocking chair, for it looks like we're in
for a long spell. Maybe, it'll be better, though, tomorrow -- always hoping.
Sure has got me worried though. But as
Evelyn and I decided, we don't want this
old system patched up- we'd rather have
something entirely new.

Had lunch today with Eliz. H, Helen H and
Lee Ola. Then Lee Ola came back to the

January 27, 1936: A manuscript back from *Husbands*.

April 8, 1936: This date brings me to the end of 5 long years of writing, the trial time I allowed myself. Balancing the books, I find 3 stories sold as follows:

You're Telling Me, *Birmingham News*, $10.

Fragment of Love, *Thrilling Love*, $55.

Beyond the Bend, *Thrilling Love*, $45:

An excerpt from "Beyond the Bend":

The next thing she knew his arms were about her, drawing her to him. She felt his breath on her cheek; then, lips pressed passionately to hers. She could feel the subtle steel of his muscles tightening about her, the press of his body close against hers. She glimpsed ecstasy for a long, thrilling moment.

As quickly as it had happened it was over. Bruce released her.

"We just had to celebrate," he murmured apologetically, then wheeled and hurried down the walk. At the gate he turned, called softly, "Good night, Peggy."

Even in Elizabeth's short stories, sex goes only so far.

WHILE ELIZABETH STRUGGLES to master the pulp formula, the world beyond Roebuck Springs is awash in great love stories. In April 1936, Edward VIII gives up the throne of England for Wallis Simpson. In 1937, the quartet of Scarlett, Rhett, Melanie, and Ashley takes the nation by storm; within six months after its publication, *Gone With the Wind* sells its first million copies. During 1936, Elizabeth does not sell a single story.

ELIZABETH: How that woman [Vera Brittain] wrote that book [*Honorable Estate*] is beyond me. Given all the days of my life to devote to it, I could never do it. I've just no talent . . .

A rare moment of truth.

Yet Elizabeth makes a timid New Year's Resolution:

*To sell two stories. Is that being too hopeful?*

Elizabeth and Stewart decide to collaborate on a novel. Elizabeth helps think up the plot, reads copy, types and retypes numerous drafts. Only Stewart's name appears on the final manuscript. Elizabeth never complains about this. They hire a New York agent, John Blassingame.

ELIZABETH: January 7, 1936: Where in God's name do we get the $15 to send to J. B.?

Blassingame submits their novel to *Country Gentleman*.

ELIZABETH: While they did not accept it, they wrote a very nice letter asking to see future work.

They write a murder mystery entitled "Striptease Dancer," set in New Orleans.

ELIZABETH: J. B. blasted the hell out of it.

A BIG LITERARY Figure comes to Birmingham: Clifton Fadiman, book editor for the *New Yorker* and reviewer for *The Nation*, known in the publishing trade as the Lord High Executioner among reviewers. A colleague on the *New Yorker* describes Fadiman:

*Born sneering.*

Stewart manages to meet this Eastern sophisticate. They have a few drinks. Stewart talks about serving with Pershing on the Mexican border, about taking a fellow ambulance driver to the hospital in Italy. Fadiman, perhaps under the illusion that he has met up with an undiscovered Ernest Hemingway, makes an unusual offer: he will read Stewart's new manuscript about his struggles to become a writer.

In no time at all, compared to paid agents, the Lord High Executioner gives it to Stewart straight.

Fadiman's letter to Stewart:

No publisher will touch it as a book . . . writers who have failed are legion . . . they won't want to read about another writer who has . . . It's perfectly true that the writing game is a tough one; no one should try freelancing full time unless he has a real gift or a made-to-order formula (Octavus Cohen, for instance.) Even a good pulp man makes damn little money and slaves to make it. Hell, I never encourage writers: I've seen too many lives in past wasted.

Fadiman embarks on a new venture, a radio program, Information Please, packed with general information, quips, comments, and—a reviewer says—wit and erudition. He has no further time to waste on failed writers.

ELIZABETH AND STEWART do not fail as writers for lack of trying. All those nights in their claw-sets trying to master formulas for Westerns and thrilling love stories. Stewart never finishes the book he started in 1918 about transporting the dead, the dying, and the maimed in his ambulance on the Italian front; meantime Ernest Hemingway, the gravely injured fellow driver whom he transported to a hospital, captures this scene in *A Farewell to Arms*.

While Stewart embroiders his brief stints in the West, readers are gobbling up books about the South . . . the benighted South of Erskine Caldwell's *Tobacco Road*, T. S. Stribling's *The Store*, and William Faulkner's Snopses trilogy; the racist South of Richard Wright's *Native Son*; the swampy South of Marjorie Kinnan Rawlings's *The Yearling*; the Appalachian South of Thomas Wolfe's *Look Homeward Angel*; towering above them all, the romanticized South of Margaret Mitchell's *Gone With the Wind*.

John Steinbeck, in *The Grapes of Wrath*, makes the Okies into a metaphor for all whose lives are destroyed by tragic circumstances that they are powerless to control. But Elizabeth and Stewart shrink from writing about how the Great Depression—accentuated by the Great Fear and High Romanticism—has devastated them and their family.

While Thomas Wolfe is spilling his guts in *You Can't Go Home Again* and *Of Time and the River*, Elizabeth and Stewart refuse to reveal their innermost lives. Why—for starters—do both still live at home with their parents? Why did Elizabeth so quickly recoil from marriage? Why is Stewart, on the cusp of forty, still a bachelor?

Elizabeth: Stewart has at last come to the realization (not new to me) that hard work and time will not bring him publishing success. He's toying with what to do next . . . what to do? What to do? Perhaps after all we are both meant to be just ordinary human beings, destined to lead usual lives with no money, no fame, no success along any line.

Addendum: Don't despair, Elizabeth. Keep plugging away; you'll get a break.

Elizabeth: October 23, 1939: This is a great day. Got a check for $70 from *Love Story* . . . was in a daze all week . . . almost twice as much as I expected to get. Much has happened since I last wrote . . . even war [in Europe] has been declared!

January 24, 1940:

Another story sale . . . "Love Blackout" to Standard Magazines [publisher of a group of thirty magazines including *Thrilling Love, Thrilling Detectives, Thrilling Western*]. Check $45. I can't take in the fact that I've actually got $46 in the bank and a few extra dollars in my purse, enough to take someone to lunch without having to go into an economical tailspin . . . These two sales have changed my entire outlook on life.

February 10, 1939:

Stewart's book came out titled *Death for the Lady*. He is Birmingham's newest celebrity and everybody is talking about it and him . . . he has had 3 or 4 newspaper notices . . . J. T. Graves's column . . . Childers's page . . . and The Wanderer column . . . We are delighted the way readers seem to like it. Even Ted says S. deserves a better publisher than Phoenix.

# Our Summer Trip

L ed by Father, we travel wherever automobiles can take us and bring us home within two weeks. It never occurs to us to travel by any means other than fully loaded automobile. Ship voyages are for the wealthy; airplanes for risk-takers like Charles Lindbergh and Amelia Earhart. For people in ordinary circumstances, Europe is as unattainable as the moon, except in the event of a world war (as in Stewart's case).

Dorothy and Ted have their annual disagreement: what will be our sole luxury of the current year—new dining room furniture (Dorothy's heart's desire) or a summer trip? As usual, Father gets his way.

During the winter months, he selects the route and plans each day's itinerary. He will do all the driving in a black Ford, the Locomobile, or, when things look up, a Chrysler New Yorker. Elizabeth, appointing herself the navigator, keeps track of our progress in a five-cent, spiral-bound notebook: what time we depart each morning, what time we arrive at our destination, total miles covered, and, almost incidentally, sights seen. I watch for state lines in my eagerness to collect at filling stations a new decal to glue on the back windshield. Miss Rose scans the horizon anxiously.

Obviously there are no mountains ahead as we cross a narrow, two-lane strip of blacktop between Miami and the west coast of Florida. Nonetheless, Miss Rose begins to scribble on an envelope as best she can in the crowded back seat. She has seen a sign denoting this road as Alligator Alley.

*What are you doing, Mama?*

Miss Rose, defiantly: *Writing my will!*

Moments later, with a loud bang, a tire blows out. Father manages to keep the car from careening into a ditch that may well be home to an alligator.

*Left, on the running board of the Locomobile—Daytona beach. Right, what the average travelers wore in the 1930s. From left, Miss Rose, Elizabeth, Dorothy, and Ted, at Mount Vernon.*

Miss Rose, triumphant:

*You see, Teddy, I knew we wouldn't make it!*

To Father's way of thinking, it is a mortal sin to leave a seat vacant in a car headed for interesting places. Thus he never travels without five (preferably six) passengers crammed shoulder to shoulder, hip to hip, each with one small suitcase in the trunk.

How do we stand the hot, humid air that assaults us through the open windows of a car moving at fifty miles an hour—clad as we are in dresses, various undergarments, silk stockings, hats and, in Miss Rose's case, a veil and gloves; Father in long-sleeved shirt, tie, seersucker suit, and straw boater, its inner band stained with sweat? For the most part, we female family members are conditioned to endure hardships without complaint. If our leader decrees a 450-mile day along main streets and two-lane highways in the era before air-conditioned cars, so be it.

But on one disastrous occasion, Father's generosity backfires. Elizabeth cannot go; finances are too tight. So he invites Ronald and Libba, a newlywed couple in straitened circumstances who regard this free trip as their honeymoon. To Father's frustration, the honeymooners are never sitting on their suitcases at the prescribed (usually 7 A.M.) departure hour for the day's trip. How dare Ronald and Libba defy Father's marching orders! It never occurs to me to surmise why they are always tardy.

We venture out of the Deep South on three major highways. If headed toward Chicago, we drive U.S. 31, officially called the Beeline but more ominously known as Bloody 31 for its heavy toll of accidents. On a trip to California we pick up U.S.

66, joining the hegira of "Okies" fleeing the Dust Bowl for that fabled land of milk and honey. To cross the Mojave Desert, we get up at 4 A.M. and, indulging in a rare luxury, rent a primitive form of air-conditioning attached to a back window. This "swamp cooler" blows hot air through the car, dropping inside temperatures from, say, 110 degrees to a mere 95 degrees. Arriving in Los Angeles, we rent an apartment so that we can cook our own meals. However, we splurge once at a cafeteria, its fountain spouting free lemonade and its walls adorned with promises of life eternal. Miss Rose is enchanted.

But most summers find us setting forth south on U.S. 11 (the Lee Highway in Tennessee and Virginia), headed south toward New Orleans or north toward the Great Smoky Mountains, the historic shrines of the Old Dominion and Washington, or the 1939 New York World's Fair. (On recent travels, I tend to forget almost instantly the designations of modern freeways—had that been I-24, I-40 or I-81?—but, half a century after the trips of my childhood, the numbers 31, 66 and 11 remain firmly fixed in my memory.)

U.S. 11 bears us from Birmingham directly along the main streets of small Southern towns and cities. On both sides of this intimate road, a stream of entrepreneurs importune us to buy gaudy chenille bedspreads—even a double bed version of the Stars and Bars of the Confederacy—as well as a host of other adornments. To enhance the front lawn, why not a little black groom, hand extended to grasp the reins of an imaginary horse, or a fountain shaped like a small boy, water trickling from a part of the male anatomy normally hidden from my view? To adorn the mantel, would we like an original oil painting in our choice of subjects—lion, snowcapped mountain, or the self-taught artist's conception of Jesus?

Other temptations soon beset us. Dozens of red birdhouses advertise "See Seven States From Rock City." Barn roofs bear larger messages: "Discover the Lost Sea" and "Explore Sequoyah Caverns Finest Cave or Your Money Back." As we cross a corner of Georgia, someone offers "Blood Test for Marriage: No Waiting"—a message over which I puzzle in silence—and the proprietor of a "game park" urges us to see a half-buffalo-half-cow, a horse with ski feet, and an old-fashioned Texas electric chair.

After U.S. 11 rounds the Moccasin Bend of the Tennessee River at Chattanooga, we begin a maddeningly slow passage through small east Tennessee towns swarming with Saturday shoppers. Tent revivals, Bible colleges, and other

*New Orleans. Dorothy, left, and Virginia.*

manifestations of Southern fundamentalism line this portion of the highway. White letters on rocks proclaim, "Jesus Is Soon Coming. Are You Ready?" or warn "Get Right With God."

Around noon, I begin to pay particular attention to those merchants proffering catfish, barbecue, pecan candy, Grapette, cherry cider, R. C. Cola, and a variety of other delights to Southern taste buds. But of necessity we resist these roadside sirens as determinedly as we had the purveyors of bedspreads, fountains, and oil paintings. At some roadside table, close by exhaust fumes from passing traffic, Miss Rose unveils waxed-paper parcels of stuffed eggs and ham sandwiches. Dorothy produces collapsible aluminum cups and a big silver thermos of coffee or tea. Another ritual inevitably follows this repast: Miss Rose's arch announcement that she wishes to wash her hands. This necessitates a stop at a filling station carefully selected for its promise of a clean ladies' room. Reared in the South, we take it for granted that all such doors bear the warning "whites only."

U.S. 11 passes right by Andrew Johnson's tailor shop in Greeneville, Tennessee, directly over Virginia's Natural Bridge; down the main street of Lexington, Virginia, one block from the cold recumbent statue of Robert E. Lee and from my chief interest, Stonewall Jackson's stuffed horse—had not the great Stonewall, in his Valley campaign of 1862, galloped Little Sorrell up and down this very road?—and within sight of the birthplace in Staunton of Miss Rose's hero, Woodrow Wilson.

To afford this annual extravagance, we adhere to a daily budget: $1 for food and $1 for lodging apiece. One dollar suffices to buy three plain but ample meals in small-town cafes or big-city cafeterias. (We pack lunch only on the first day.) Housewives in frame Victorians along U.S. 11 supplement their family incomes by hanging out the handmade sign "Tourist Home" and renting clean but sometimes lumpy beds in spare rooms for $1 a person. My own preference in lodging runs to the newest thing: a row of tiny wooden structures lighted at night by the red neon sign "Tourist Cabins."

However, in Abingdon, Virginia, we stumble across what appears, at first, to be a night of rare luxury—a large, red brick inn, just converted from a girls' boarding school named, rather grandiosely, Martha Washington College. To our surprise, the room rate fits our budget.

Miss Rose, Elizabeth, and I follow a young man, bowed under the weight of three suitcases, to the room we are to share. With a flourish, the bellhop flings open the door to a sleeping porch with twenty narrow cots! Miss Rose is momentarily speechless; Elizabeth and I collapse in giggles. What we do not know—until the following day—is that Martha Washington College had shut down because its students—including recent occupants of the hard cots on which we had passed the night—had fled an epidemic of typhoid fever.

That evening, we attend George Bernard Shaw's *Major Barbara* at a nearby theater where anyone who lacks forty cents—as a lot of people do—can trade home-grown fruits and vegetables for admission. In return for food, unemployed Broadway actors offer entertainment. Robert Porterfield, who came up with the idea of this Barter Theater, recompenses authors with Virginia's famous country hams. What Shaw, an ardent vegetarian, received in lieu of royalties we do not learn. Turnip greens, perhaps.

*Major Barbara* is a welcome distraction. On most of our nightly stopovers, there is absolutely nothing to do but eat at the nearest cafeteria, Lux our undies and silk stockings, and try to fall asleep in some hot bedroom. As each day dawns, Miss Rose, fearful that her daughter or granddaughter might see her unclothed—and determined to be ready on time—is rustling around, getting dressed.

For a fifteen-day vacation (not requiring overnight accommodations on the last night), each person's basic expenses come to twenty-nine dollars, with perhaps two or three dollars extra squirreled away for souvenirs, admissions or special treats. Our trips having taken place long before the advent of the credit card, adults entrust this precious hoard to a carefully guarded purse or billfold. Father provides the car, oil and gas; at twenty cents a gallon, twenty miles to the gallon, the automobile expenses of a 2,000-mile trip must have come to around twenty-five dollars.

By sheer endurance and rigid discipline, we cover vast distances in two weeks and see wondrous sights:

Thomas Jefferson's beloved Monticello (on a hilltop, Father is pleased to note); Jamestown, Williamsburg, the White House,

*Virginia on the lawn of George Washington's home, Mount Vernon, overlooking the Potomac River.*

the Capitol, the Washington Monument, the Lincoln Memorial.

On another trip: the Empire State Building, the Statue of Liberty, Niagara Falls. On another: Grand Canyon, Big Sur, Alcatraz, giant redwoods, Yosemite Falls and Half Dome, the Donner Pass through the Rockies (Father to Miss Rose: *Just shut your eyes, Mama*), the Great Salt Lake.

These travels set me even further apart from most of my classmates whose parameters are limited, by necessity or choice, to Gatlinburg, Tennessee, on the north and Panama City, Florida, on the south.

Around dusk on a Saturday, two weeks after we set out, we make it home. Early next morning, Father sets me to the task of scraping off the state decals with a straight-edged razor blade.

That evening, he summons an audience from the neighborhood, perhaps a few friends from town. Someone makes the expected request:

*Now tell about the trip!*

Elizabeth: *We left home at 6:15 A.M. . . . .*

Father: *Now, Elizabeth, I'll tell it.*

FIFTEEN YEARS AFTER she left with her parents for Oklahoma, Elizabeth visits New Orleans. She sees her old beau:

> ELIZABETH: Was he a mess! Ugly and with a hangover or still drunk . . .
> he entertained us with Negro and drunk stories for two hours. This trip,
> if it did nothing else, certainly wrote finis to that episode. We speak a
> different language.

Elizabeth finds her Kappa Kappa Gamma "sisters" substantially and conventionally married; full of talk about houses, children, and Mardi Gras. She tries to portray her life as colorful but the Kappas see right through this stratagem:

Kappas: *You and Stewart hunt possums? How unusual!*

Whisper: *Do you suppose they eat them?*

Kappas: *So you're an author, Elizabeth. Aren't you smart!*

Whisper: *What on earth does Elizabeth know about love? Have you ever in your life heard of* Thrilling Love *magazine?*

Kappas: *Tell us, Elizabeth, how does it feel to be part of the business world?*

Whisper: *Poor thing! Did you see her fingernails?*

# Vaudeville, Picture Shows, and Other Pleasures

I t's Saturday and we're headed downtown. Miss Rose, Elizabeth, and Uvvy are all dolled up: second-best dresses, silk stockings, high heels, hats, gloves. I, too, wear my second-best dress with my black patent leathers and white socks. We are bound to run into people we know.

We pay our nickel fares and board streetcar number twenty-five that will take us downtown on the fastest route, First Avenue. We leave the familiar structures of East Lake Park—its two-block roller coaster, ferris wheel, Tunnel of Love, and House of Mirrors. We never venture to the north side of this park; Stewart, coming home late one night, actually saw the flaming crosses and white-robed figures of the Ku Klux Klan klavern that regularly meets here.

In a neighborhood called Avondale, we pass a cotton mill surrounded by the narrow shotgun houses and outdoor privies of its workers. We hear the sharp clack of wooden shuttles, the hum of looms. Then number twenty-five makes a slow climb up First Avenue viaduct, taking us safely above Sloss Furnace.

As always, we check out Birmingham's two big department stores. In Pizitz, we see Mr. Louis Pizitz himself, who came South as a peddler with a pack on his back, pacing the aisles like an aging lion, his head with its shock of white hair clearly visible above the counters. Mr. Pizitz is checking on his clerks whom he calls "my girls."

We roam Loveman's first floor, ogling perfumes, lotions, purses, silk stockings. On special occasions, we climb the stairs that lead to the tearoom on Loveman's balcony, hoping to see and be seen atop this eminence.

For us to purchase a dress ($7.95) or a pair of shoes ($2.97) at Loveman's is

*Elizabeth in favorite hat.*

out of the question. So we stroll through the ten-cent stores; at Kress, Uvvy buys curtain rings; at Woolworth's I am allowed to pick out some treat such as those ill-fated, twenty-five-cent goldfish.

In the late afternoon, Father meets us at the Studio Book Shop. We browse over Gottie's newest acquisitions until time for that rarest of treats: a non-home-cooked meal.

Since this is not Monday night, when the Britling Cafeteria offers entire dinners for eleven to nineteen cents a person, we go to the cozy basement restaurant next door to Gottie's bookstore; I love Mary Beard's thin pancakes covered with chicken hash. Although we are gathered around a table for five, Miss Rose informs the puzzled waitress:

*Give me my own ticket. I'm not with these people!*

We cannot dawdle over our second serving of pancakes (covered with syrup for dessert) because we must get to the picture show before the prices rise at 6 P.M.: at the Strand, for example, from ten cents to twenty cents.

As we come within sight of the marquee, Miss Rose breaks into a trot. She is intent on paying her own way.

Father protests: *Now Mama . . .*

In vain.

If just Elizabeth and I are going to the picture show, she lets me pick it out. I choose Johnny Weismuller in a loin cloth and Maureen O'Sullivan in flimsy rags swinging from trees in Africa. If there is no Tarzan film in town, I settle for the Marx Brothers; I laugh so hard at *Duck Soup* that I wet my pants.

Miss Rose is attracted to glamorous films, provided they contain little or no sex; Fred Astaire and Ginger Rogers in *Top Hat*, for example. But on one memorable occasion, the three of us stare in amazement as Clark Gable and Claudette Colbert (in *It Happened One Night*) share the same bedroom, only a sheet curtaining her side from his. Miss Rose puts on a show of outrage:

*If I had known . . .*

Father steers us to high adventures: Gable and Charles Laughton in *Mutiny on the Bounty*; Errol Flynn and Olivia de Havilland in *Captain Blood*; Leslie Howard and Merle Oberon in *The Scarlet Pimpernel*. It will be OK to talk about these shows on the streetcar going home—unlike *It Happened One Night*.

The Alabama is the biggest and fanciest theater in town, worth every penny of thirty-five cents just to gaze upon its velvet tiers and marble columns. It even has its own organist, Stanley Malatte, who grins like the Cheshire Cat as he and the Mighty Wurlitzer are propelled up from the orchestra pit. The Alabama also offers a few vaudeville acts (nothing to shock its family audience) such as comics, harmony singers, dancers, or Pepito, the Spanish clown.

When I turn fifteen, Father leads our little family group to a seedy theater that offers real vaudeville. I walk with my head down for fear that one of my classmates at Woodlawn High School will see me going into the Pantages accompanied by, of all people, my grandmother! We see dancers kick up their heels and reveal their bloomers in a revue billed as Parlez Vous Paree.

> VIRGINIA: Some show! Packed and jammed but not by the nicest people.

What is Father thinking when he escorts his innocent daughter to the Pantages? He had explained a year before when he walked me past the swinging doors on New Orleans's Bourbon Street:

*You are bound to see the seamy side of life someday, Virginia; I want you to see it first with me.*

DURING BASEBALL SEASON, we go to town on streetcar number thirty-eight that will take us within walking distance of Rickwood Field. Connie Mack himself helped design this minor league ballpark; Rickwood even boasts electric fans that send blasts of air—hot or cold depending on the weather—over spectators and players alike.

Father's other heroes—Christy Mathewson, Honus Wagner, and Babe Ruth—have played this field. But Rickwood's proudest hour occurred in 1931 when Ray Caldwell, a forty-one-year-old pitcher for the Birmingham Barons, out-pitched none other than Dizzy Dean (who had guaranteed victory for his Houston Buffalos); the Barons won 1-0.

Father and I know all the Baron players because we faithfully follow their games over our Philco radio. "The Voice of the Barons" embroiders the bare facts as they come across the ticker tape. I know his signature lines well enough to chant along with him:

*Three and two! Wot's he gonna do?*
*Did you hear that?*

*There he goes! He's O_U_T_T_T!*

(Who could ever have imagined that this brash sportscaster, Eugene Connor, whom we all call "Bull", will play such an infamous role in the civil rights battles to come?)

In the fall, West End offers other attractions. The State Fair assembles on the fairgrounds; its midway is filled with freaks—Siamese twins; the Fat Lady and her husband, the Midget; the Bearded Lady; the Half-Man-Half-Alligator; humans with six fingers or eight toes. I am not allowed to enter these sideshows but I can't avoid seeing the big posters as we stroll down the sawdust aisles; I even glimpse the Fan Dancer cleverly waving her white ostrich feathers.

At Legion Field, home of Alabama's Crimson Tide, Coach Frank Thomas is racking up victories. His stars, Paul "Bear" Bryant and the passing combination of Millard "Dixie" Howell to Don Hutson, lead the Tide to victory over Stanford in the 1934 Rose Bowl. I go to a few Tide games with other girls from Woodlawn High: we shriek: *Howell to Hutson!*

How lucky we feel to live in a state with such immortals.

IT'S NIGHT BY the time we board number twenty-five headed back toward the Loop. Sloss Furnace lets loose a river of molten pig iron; even protected by the streetcar, we feel its heat. Avondale Mill village lies in darkness, its morning workers already in their beds. But the cotton mill itself glows with blue lights, its night shift moving about like shadows.

*Our lifelines to downtown: on the end of the row, numbers 38 and 25, at the car barn, 1928. Courtesy of Birmingham Public Library Archives.*

# PART FIVE

# *We Make It Through*

# Ted Gets His Pulpit

J udging by outward appearances, Ted has overcome the Great Fear. Through
his work with the Van der Veer Company, he makes new friends in town.
He volunteers to work for the Birmingham Community Chest; he and others talk about founding a symphony orchestra. From cosmopolitan New
York, Joe Cookman writes:

*Here's hoping your dream of a Birmingham Symphony will become a permanent
reality.*

(That's just like Ted, Joe probably thinks—proposing to start a symphony
orchestra in destitute Birmingham, Alabama, in 1933!)

Through these activities, Ted meets James E. Chappell, editor of the *Birmingham News* and the *Birmingham Age-Herald*. He invites Jim and his wife, Corinne,
to our Sunday afternoon softball games. (They come but they don't play.) The
Chappells become regulars in Ted's evening reading group.

In January 1935, Jim Chappell names Ted associate editor and chief editorial
writer for the *Age-Herald*. At long last Ted has his pulpit. Six mornings a week,
he rides to work on the yellow streetcars alongside salesgirls, clerks, and others
on their way downtown. Using a fat, black pencil with blunt lead, he makes notes
for editorials on the flimsy, yellow "second sheets," used in the City Room for
carbon copies. Or reads the out-of-town newspapers he brought home the night
before. Like Elizabeth, who in her girlhood could name all the brands of Kentucky
bourbon, I can reel off the names of dozens of newspapers, among them, the *New
York Herald-Tribune* and *World-Telegram*, *Richmond News-Leader*, *Atlanta Consti-
tution*, *Chicago Daily News*, *Washington Star*, *Philadelphia Inquirer*, *Boston Globe*,
*Miami Daily News*, *Des Moines Register*, *Houston Post*, *Cleveland Plain-Dealer*,
*Pittsburgh Post-Gazette*, and, of course, Father's old employers, the *Lexington*

*Ted returns to newspapering, 1935.*

*Herald, New Orleans Item, Kansas City Post,* and *New York Evening Post.*

When Ted finishes pecking out his daily quota of editorials, he walks a few steps down the hall to Mr. Chappell's office. He reads every editorial out loud to Mr. Chappell, who seldom makes any changes and sometimes sneaks a little nap. Mr. Chappell's okay eases Ted's old fear that he may be sued for libel.

To write editorials with absolute impartiality, Ted resolves, he must be free of all entanglements. He declines to join Rotary, Kiwanis, the Birmingham Country Club, or to serve on any board, even the symphony. He holds firm to his belief that an editorial writer can only, in good conscience, belong to his professional organizations (the American Society of Newspaper Editors, the Alabama Press Association) and to his church.

However, Father does not turn down the fringe benefits of his modest salary—passes and due bills. No need for us to worry anymore about whether we have twenty cents apiece for a picture show or a quarter to enter the gates of the Alabama State Fair. As if equipped with a magic wand, we sweep with our passes into Legion Field to cheer for the Crimson Tide or into Rickwood Field to watch the Barons play the Cincinnati Reds, the St. Louis Cardinals, or some major league team passing through town just ahead of the season.

But passes pale in comparison with "due bills," the custom under which the *Age-Herald* swaps free advertising space for free housing at hotels. As an editor, Father is entitled to use due bills. No more one dollar per-night-per-person spare bedrooms in hot, dingy tourist homes; now we luxuriate in big hotels like the Essex House in New York City and the Roney Plaza at Miami Beach.

When parking meters are installed in downtown Birmingham, Father and I find a little red flag on the meter by our space. Our time has expired but there is no ticket and no policeman in sight. I am all for jumping in the car and rushing away. But Father feeds the meter what he owes: ten pennies. Why, I demand to know. Father explains, as he has in many other situations: *No one can corrupt me but myself.* I dare not press the matter any further. Father might decide that he is being corrupted by the passes and the due bills.

The *Age-Herald* is a morning newspaper; its readers—bankers, realtors, housewives, and the like—are not rushing to get to an early shift at a cotton mill or a coal mine or to tend a crucible of fiery iron ore. Those who leave for work at the crack of dawn read the afternoon paper, the *Birmingham News*. If, that is, they can read at all.

One circulation consultant begs Ted to write as if all his readers have only a fourth-grade education. But Ted will not make his sentences shorter, his editorials briefer. He refuses to talk down to his readers. When Thomas Mann lectures in Birmingham, Ted's editorial impression of that world-famous novelist and Nobel Prize winner runs two full columns.

Even the *Age-Herald*'s elite subscribers probably do not stick with Ted's editorials to the very end. Yet, just by skimming them, readers are exposed to the words he uses most frequently: Freedom. Justice. Truth. Humanity. Service. Peace. The high-minded editorial page lends the *Age-Herald* an aura of morality. Most subscribers, being regular churchgoers, submit without protest to sermons from their daily newspaper.

Dr. Edmonds thinks that Ted's editorials deserve the Pulitzer Prize. He recommends this to Carl Ackerman, dean of Columbia University School of Journalism. But Ted does not win a Pulitzer; lofty ideals and appeals for world peace are not in fashion. The judges are looking for stronger meat.

# *The Bonus*

A new word—bonus—is causing problems during our Sunday afternoon conversations in Miss Rose's living room. Stewart and Father disagree about whether to accept a bonus for their service in the World War: Stewart, yes; Father, no.

Turn down an offer of money? What's the problem, Teddy? Father agrees with Hoover and Roosevelt that a big payout would further deepen the federal debt; also he suspects that a lot of men who do not really need the money would take their bonuses anyway. He didn't go into the Navy for money, Father argues; he went to serve his country.

But we *do* need the money, Stewart insists. You have a job, Ted, with a regular salary, but Dad, Elizabeth, and I are still struggling to keep our little business afloat. Secretly I side with Stewart: what luxuries we might suddenly acquire if Father would only take his bonus: a furnace for our house, the long-desired new dining room furniture, or a new winter coat for Dorothy so that I no longer will be slightly ashamed to be seen with my mother on Third Avenue.

We hear a lot about the bonus over the radio: the Senate passes it; the House passes it; Roosevelt vetoes it; Congress passes it over the President's veto. Hooray, Stewart says, he can't wait to get his hands on his share!

ELIZABETH June, 1936: Passed Bonus yesterday. Traded the old Ford on a used 1934 model V-8 De Luxe car that is a beauty!

Mac, in one of his silent moods, does not say a word about the new car but Elizabeth thinks that he likes it. Whatever is left after he buys the 1934 Ford V-8, Stewart puts into the family business. Father does not take the bonus. I never hear my mother complain about this or lament her lack of a new coat and dining room furniture. Father never says another word about this subject but I suspect that he is silently reciting his mantra: *no one can corrupt me but myself.*

# *Matters of Faith*

Eloquent though he is, even Dr. Henry M. Edmonds cannot keep restless Miss Rose in his congregation every Sunday. Insofar as religion is concerned, she is born to shop.

In Frankfort, Miss Rose was reared as a Presbyterian in a church still divided between Union and Confederate sympathizers. She married the handsome baritone soloist, thereby lining up with the Unionists. Distraught after the death of Baby Eleanor, she took up Ella Wheeler Wilcox's popular New Thought with its thesis that the mind could mold the body.

In New Orleans, she sneaked out of the Presbyterian fold to dabble in Christian Science and Unitarianism. In Kansas City, under the spell of the famous English orator Dr. Charles Aked, she joined the Congregational Church. When Dr. Aked failed to meet her needs, she attended a neighborhood center of the Unity movement, a faith-healing and reincarnation cult founded by Charles and Myrtle Fillmore.

In Birmingham, Dr. Edmonds being at the height of his popularity, Miss Rose—attracted as always to the unconventional—reverts at least formally to Presbyterianism. Dr. Edmonds had founded in 1915 a new church named, appropriately, the Independent Presbyterian Church. His congregants followed him out of his original pastorate, split by a raging controversy over the literal interpretation of the Bible.

Dr. Edmonds rejects the traditional Presbyterian doctrine of total depravity and even dares to question the Virgin Birth and Resurrection as not requisite to the divinity of Jesus Christ. His new church adopts the so-called Social Gospel of outreach to the less fortunate. Many fellow ministers shun Dr. Edmonds because he does not fulminate in behalf of Prohibition and strict observance of the

Sabbath. Members of Dr. Edmonds's congregation may, if they choose, drink in moderation any evening or play golf on Sunday (in our case, softball) without fear of eternal damnation.

Furthermore, with the Scopes "monkey" trial and the trials of the Scottsboro Boys inflaming emotions worldwide, Dr. Edmonds preaches against religious and racial antagonisms. He regards science and religion as partners, not competitors.

Quote from one of Dr. Edmonds's sermons in the 1920s:

> Religion and science are thus two pilgrims on their way to the city of our God. What a pity that they can not agree on their journey. The direction is the same, the goal is the same and each is dependent on the other. True we may have science without religion and we may have religion without science. But either deprived of the other is but half itself. Without science we should have a world without an explanation and without a method of dealing with it . . . Science deals with the seen, religion with the unseen. Science deals with the temporal, religion with the eternal . . .

Dr. Edmonds also passionately opposes modern warfare; from her front pew Miss Rose nods her vigorous approval.

One would think that Miss Rose would settle down, content with Dr. Edmonds and his unorthodox views. Not so. Like any addict, she searches for stronger, more exotic dosages. Accompanied by the compliant Elizabeth, she goes to Municipal Auditorium to hear Toyohiko Kagawa, a Japanese evangelist and pacifist. Kagawa disappoints.

> ELIZABETH: I can't imagine from whence cometh [Kagawa's] power as I found him quite juvenile . . .

Thence to philosophers from India. Miss Rose discovers the writings of Aurobindo Ghose, known to his followers as Sri Aurobindo, who seeks to transform the world by creating a disciplined religious elitism, and of the theosophist Jiddu Krishnamurti, who also appears in Birmingham. Elizabeth accompanies her mother to hear Krishnamurti, speaking on someone's lawn, explain his belief in transmigration of the soul.

On some Sundays, they go to a downtown hotel to hear proponents of Bahaism preach religious unity, equality of men and women, and—Miss Rose's favorite cause—world peace. At other times, to meetings of a group calling itself The Infinite Way. Etc. . . . etc. . . . ad infinitum.

In what she called their "little talks," Miss Rose tried to steer her favorite child toward a career in the church.

> Ted: When I was a small boy, I was told and half believed I was intended for the ministry but as I grew older, I became frightened; fear took the place of assurance and I began to creep back into myself rather than to wedge my way into the life of others.

It must have been about this time that Teddy began to beg his father to excuse him from reciting in front of his classmates at the Friday afternoon exercises at school.

As an adult, Ted does not roam, like his mother, from one religion to the next: he joins the Independent Presbyterian Church. He agrees with practically everything Dr. Edmonds says, but he is not a regular churchgoer. He does not say the blessing at meals. He does not have his young daughter baptized. Father's beliefs transcend mere formalities of church or creed.

Take, for example, this occurrence in later years.

> Dr. Edmonds's successor: Ted, this is the first time in my memory that the boards of our church—the deacons and the elders—have each chosen the same person to join their ranks. So which invitation do you accept?

> Ted: I must decline to serve in either capacity because I cannot in good conscience recite the Apostles' Creed; I do not literally believe certain portions.

Father spends his Sunday mornings on the porch or by the fireside, seeking answers to the ultimate mysteries from philosophers at the highest level of neoorthodox theology. He is not only searching for the meaning of life. He is looking to God to help him conquer the Great Fear that has blighted his early promise and almost devastated his life. If one fears life, he tells himself, he is distrusting God who brought him into being.

With the help of the philosophers, Father formulates his own creed:

*Love God and seek His presence and His will.*

*Love thy neighbors. Extend meaningful relations with others.*

*Increase control over thoughts, emotions, moods.*

*Abandon self to God. Live in the midst of life. Do not try to escape.*

*The Independent Presbyterian Church. Perhaps our family arrived on an occasional Sunday in one of those cars. Other members could come to church via a Highland Avenue streetcar. Courtesy of the Birmingham Public Library Archives.*

# Dear President Hoover

Miss Rose spends long days alone. Elizabeth, Stewart, and Mac take the family Ford to work but, even if she had a car, Miss Rose would not know how to drive it. The cook of the moment repairs to the servant's quarters for a snooze. After Miss Rose orders her groceries by telephone, she has no one else to talk to.

Miss Rose has no close friends, Hen'retta Blackburn, Birdie Brown, and the other comrades of her youth being far away in Kentucky. Her Alabama neighbors—who know nothing of Dr. John Harvey Kellogg, Dr. Charles Aked, or Mary Baker Eddy—titter at the sight of Miss Rose's purple hair and white winter coat. When her staid sister comes to visit, Auntie expresses her vocal disapproval of everything in sight: her nephew hunting possums, her unmarried niece writing love stories for cheap magazines, both still living at home. To Auntie's way of thinking, when Rose chose Mac instead of a doctor or a lawyer, she got her just desserts.

How better to pass the long days than by writing letters in behalf of world peace? If another war breaks out, her sons—even though in their mid-forties—might be put in harm's way a second time. Miss Rose's hero in the cause of peace, Woodrow Wilson, is long dead. She suspects Franklin Roosevelt of being a devious warmonger. So she raises this issue with the person she considers the one "sane" leader, former President Herbert Hoover.

Miss Rose suggests that Hoover be the 1940 Republican presidential nominee on a peace and League of Nations platform; only he, she says, can keep the United States from being "Roosevelt-ridden until the end of time." In a P.S., she begs: "Please answer."

From his suite in the Waldorf-Astoria, the former President—who has confessed to the press that he has nothing much to do except cut ribbons and take pills—does indeed answer politely but noncommittally. He encloses an article he has written for the *Atlantic Monthly*.

Miss Rose is thrilled with her new pen pal. She sends Hoover copies of Teddy's editorials; her son, "who lives on a mountain not far from me" knows nothing, she assures Hoover, of his mother's correspondence. She suggests that the 1940 Republican convention be held after the Democratic convention has decided whether or not to nominate FDR for a third term.

> Rose Stewart Van der Veer to Herbert Hoover
> July 28, 1938
> . . . is there a law for the Democrats to hold [their convention] last? I'd like to know!!

Miss Rose informs Hoover that she was reared in Kentucky; she invokes the old, magic names—John Young Brown, J. C. S. Blackburn, W. C. P. Breckinridge, Henry Watterson. Only for business reasons, she assures Hoover, have she and her family settled in the "benighted pine woods state" of Alabama.

> Herbert Hoover to Rose Stewart Van der Veer:
> August 3, 1938
> . . . I greatly appreciate your most kind expressions . . .

Their correspondence continues sporadically as the thirties wind down. Eventually even Miss Rose concludes that Hoover's platitudes will not stave off war. She casts a wider net:

> H. V. Kaltenborn to Rose Stewart Van der Veer:
> November 5, 1938
> . . . We are not as far apart as you think.

> Charles A. Beard to Rose Stewart Van der Veer:
> April 2, 1939
> . . . glad to note that [your son and other Southern newspapers] are also opposing our rushing headlong into war.

> Dorothy Thompson to Rose Stewart Van der Veer:

November 24, 1941

...I was indeed glad that both you and your son enjoyed my columns...

Less than a month after she receives this letter from Dorothy Thompson, Miss Rose, Teddy, and other American isolationists will hear the shocking news that dooms their hopes.

# A Visit To Chickamauga

The War Between the States, as my schoolmates and I are taught to call it, is a presence in our lives, this war of our great-grandfathers more vivid to us than the Great War of 1917–18 in which our fathers fought. If we are too impatient to say The War Between the States, we simply say the War; no one mistakes our meaning. The War, or so it seems, ended just days ago; one of my teachers, after describing the burning of Atlanta and Sherman's March to the Sea, heaves a mighty sigh of relief and pronounces:

*Thank goodness, that's all over now!*

Actually, for Southerners, the War is not over; just the fighting.

My own sympathies lie unreservedly with the Confederacy; Robert E. Lee, Stonewall Jackson, and J. E. B. Stuart are my heroes. When Roland and I play with his lead soldiers, I never really resent it if Roland, executing clever maneuvers, carries the day for the troops in gray.

At Robinson School, our history books are filled with accounts of General Nathan Bedford Forrest ("The Wizard of the Saddle") whose 600 Confederate cavalrymen fooled the Yankees into surrendering to their much smaller force; of brave, sixteen-year-old Emma Sansom, who showed General Forrest a shallow ford where he and his men could cross Black Creek; of Joseph ("Fightin' Joe") Wheeler, whose dashing career as a cavalry leader began at Shiloh when he was twenty-five, and of Major John Pelham (called "Gallant Pelham" by Lee himself) who gave his life for the Confederacy at twenty-four. Not much, if anything, about brave, gallant, fighting men in blue.

At home we never talk about the War. Nowadays Daddy Mac seldom talks about anything. Miss Rose and Father have no time to waste on an old war; they are too busy trying to stave off a new one. Father struggles daily to convince read-

*Yankees—*
*what a shock!*

ers of the *Age-Herald* to remain calm, resist impulsive actions, and strive to keep the peace. Miss Rose clips these editorials and mails them to Herbert Hoover, H. V. Kaltenborn, Dorothy Thompson, et al.

So, when we set off on a day trip at 5 A.M. one Sunday, I have no inkling as to what lies ahead. From my childhood battles with Roland, I retain a vague idea of the maneuvers at Shiloh, Gettysburg, and Fredericksburg. But Roland and I never played Chickamauga.

I might have suspected something unusual: Miss Rose always goes on trips; Daddy Mac never. But today she stays home; Daddy Mac sits silently in the front seat, his black fedora hiding his baldness.

It's damp and chilly, much like it was on those two days in September 1863 when this battle raged. As we drive slowly through Chickamauga National Military Park, Uvvy and I huddle together in the back seat of our unheated car. There's nobody else around. With dense wood and heavy underbrush on either side, this field of battle—except for monuments and markers—looks almost as it did a century ago.

Father spies a certain green marker. We pile out on the rain-soaked soil. It reads, in part: *Thirty-Fifth Ohio Infantry. Van Derveer's Brigade. Brannan's Division. Thomas' Corps.*

One word on that marker stuns me: Ohio! All our front porch talk about the past has focused on Kentucky and New Orleans; no one even mentioned Ohio. Too painful, probably, for Mac to recall.

We find a lot of other markers tracing the movements of Van Derveer's Brigade. Finally we get out of the car and walk to the crest of Snodgrass Hill. Here stands a large, stone monument bearing a bronze medallion of Colonel Ferdinand Van Derveer, Daddy Mac's uncle. On the opposite side of this monument, a tablet lists the names of those under Ferdinand's command, including Captain John Van Derveer who was to die of war-related illness when his eldest child was barely twelve years old.

Upon finding his father's name, Daddy Mac doesn't say anything. But, to my horror, I notice a tear rolling down his cheek. I have never before seen a grown man weep.

Having just turned fifteen, I don't dwell upon the larger implications of the discovery that my ancestors fought against slavery and for the federal union. Rather, I shudder at the thought of what my classmates at Woodlawn High School will say if they ever find out that I am, by direct descent, that most abhorred of creatures—a Yankee.

No middle name. No "yes ma'am" or "yes sir." No sisters or brothers. No blessing at the dinner table. No new dress at Easter. No baptism. And now I bear (secretly, I trust) the burden of being, to the mores of the white South, the ultimate traitor. All the way back to Birmingham, I am as silent as Daddy Mac.

IN YEARS TO COME, I am to outgrow my Confederate indoctrination; and to take pride in the cause for which my ancestors fought. I also learn about my great-great uncle Ferdinand Van Derveer.

For five hours, his men held the right flank of the Union troops that General George Thomas had positioned atop Snodgrass Hill. When they grew short of ammunition they raided the cartridge boxes of the dead and wounded of both sides. Exhausting this supply, they awaited the enemy with fixed bayonets.

General James Longstreet ordered thirty-five frontal assaults against this stronghold by Robert E. Lee's best fighting men from the Army of Virginia; always Thomas's men, protected only by a low line of logs, repelled the enemy. In heroism and total casualties, Longstreet's assaults would later be compared with Pickett's famous charge at Gettysburg.

Thomas, hopelessly outnumbered, finally ordered his men to withdraw. Vet-

erans of the 35th Ohio regiment would later claim that the last shots of the great battle of Chickamauga came from their guns. As twilight fell, the survivors of Brannan's division walked down a slope covered with a carpet of dry leaves and twigs—little flames burning here and there—and past the bodies of countless wounded and dead.

In two days of fighting, each side lost approximately one-third of its forces. Union and Confederate casualties combined totaled 37,129 compared with 23,582 for both armies on the single day of Antietam and 43,454 for the three days of Gettysburg.

Brannan's division sustained the highest casualties; Ferdinand Van Derveer's third brigade went into action with 1,788 men and suffered 748 (42 percent) killed and wounded, more than a third of Brannan's total losses. Although Thomas became famous as "The Rock of Chickamauga," Van Derveer's brigade had saved the Union's left flank six times. According to the *Civil War Times*, (October 2003), scholars note these actions as "one of the great combat performances of the entire war" and termed Ferdinand "the other Rock of Chickamauga."

Its victory at Chickamauga heartened the Confederacy to endure another year of war. On the Union side, the engagement meant disgrace for General William

S. Rosecrans, Commander of the Army of the Cumberland, and the loss of his command to General Thomas, who was soon placed under the Military Division of the Mississippi, commanded by then Major-General Ulysses S. Grant.

On a quiet morning in June 1888, two former Union officers rode across the fields and slopes where, twenty-five years earlier, they had taken part in the great battle. Reining in their horses on a knoll, Ferdinand Van Derveer, who had been promoted to General, and his close aide, Colonel Henry Boynton, pointed out their fighting positions. They spoke of their commanders, Rosecrans, Thomas, Brannan, and also of their former enemies led by Nathan Bedford Forrest, Ben Hardin, and, in particular, those led by Longstreet who had swept up the slopes of Snodgrass Hill like an ocean tide, receded, swept up again, losing 44 percent of their wing, most within an hour and a half on that long-ago Sunday afternoon.

They said to each other that this field should be preserved as had been Gettysburg. But, they insisted, this site should go beyond Gettysburg with its monuments, at that time, only to the Union forces. In 1890, Congress authorized the first Civil War battlefield to memorialize the courage and sacrifices of *both* sides. Ferdinand Van Derveer and Henry Boynton are honored as the founders of Chickamauga National Military Park.

Thank you, Ferdinand. You helped to open my mind.

# 1937: Climactic Year

Elizabeth:
   New Year's Eve:
   Last night S and I went 'possum hunting . . . got 2 and on the way to the car the dogs ran a coon for about an hour. The valley and creek were thick with fog. At midnight, firecrackers, guns, etc., could be heard all over the countryside. On the way home, every farm house boasted of a light. We couldn't decide whether it was New Year's Eve parties or getting up to do the milking.

Monster floods on the Ohio River at Louisville. Miss Rose orders everybody in the family to go through our closets. She packs our already worn-out clothes and sends them to the Red Cross for distribution to her fellow Kentuckians.

FEBRUARY: I AM fifteen. A senior in high school. The phone rings. It's Virgil again. I have no problem recognizing Virgil's voice; he's been calling me for three years.

   VIRGINIA: VT called again. I told him I wasn't home. Hopeless case!!
      VT called again but I was "busy" to him. Sap!

Virgil tries another method of communication.

   VIRGINIA: Got the sappiest letter from Virgil. I am his inspiration, etc. Made me want to go to the rail.

But Virgil is not a "sap." He is handsome, polite, well-mannered, an A student. I won't answer Virgil's telephone calls because I am scared to death of having a boyfriend. What would Father do if I let Virgil come to see me? What if Virgil tried to hold my hand? Put his arm around my shoulder? Kiss me?

I find a package on my desk at school in plain sight where everybody sees it and giggles. Unfortunate choice, Virgil. I love chocolate in every form except when it covers cherries. I am always disappointed if I happen to choose, from a box of candy, a chocolate-covered cherry; I hate those little rivers of sweet, red juice that gush out. Without a word to Virgil, I take the box of chocolate-covered cherries home and give it to Audrey.


JAMES WELDON JOHNSON comes to Birmingham. Father sees this announcement in a weekly column in the *Birmingham News* entitled "What Negroes Are Doing."

My parents and about fifty other whites attend Johnson's lecture sponsored by an elite organization of Negro women, the Periclean Club. Despite sparse publicity, 1,200 turn out to hear this noted poet read from his works and extol "The Creative Genius of the Negro." Father has read James Weldon Johnson's novel, *The Autobiography of an Ex-Colored Man*, and his highly acclaimed columns of poetry and free verse, including *God's Trombones*. The sponsors politely usher their white visitors to front pews so they can see and clearly hear the man named by the NAACP in 1925 as America's outstanding black.

I spend that evening at the Ritz Theater watching Merle Oberon and Brian Aherne in *Beloved Enemy*. Probably my parents never considered bringing their daughter to Johnson's reading. But not because of fears for my safety. I would have been accorded every courtesy, in contrast to the terrible fate of four young, black girls who are to die in 1963 when a bomb explodes in the Sixteenth Street

*Growing up.*

Baptist Church where James Weldon Johnson read his poetry on that peaceful night in 1937.

MARCH: LAWRENCE TIBBETT appears in concert at Phillips High School. Father persuades Daddy Mac, usually a stay-at-home in the evenings, to go with him to hear this noted baritone.

I go to the Terminal Station, stand outside, and catch a glimpse of Mrs. Franklin D. Roosevelt. (We do not refer to First Ladies by their first names.) Thousands line Fifth Avenue North

*Age sixteen, wearing a Pi Beta Phi pledge pin— and lipstick!*

and cheer as Mrs. Roosevelt passes, like a queen, in an open motorcar. These people are expressing their gratitude that her husband literally transformed their lives by giving them government jobs, refinancing mortgages on their farms and homes, bringing electricity to isolated areas, and—best of all—setting up a federal program to provide pensions for them in their old age.

Mrs. Roosevelt's auto route will take her through downtown, then to the Negro Industrial High School, where students serenade her with "Swing Low, Sweet Chariot," and to inspect a federal housing project for Negroes. Watch it, Mrs. Roosevelt: many more stopovers like those two and your popularity hereabouts will take a dive.

APRIL: ON SATURDAYS when I ride the streetcar downtown to shop at Loveman's and go to a picture show, I wear my new black straw hat with a tiny veil. And, just like Miss Rose, I put on my white gloves. I have outgrown Shirley Temple, Zazu Pitts, even the Marx Brothers. My new favorites are Jean Arthur of the squeaky voice; Grace Moore, cool and untouchable, and haughty Katherine Hepburn. But I tend to choose movies based chiefly on leading men—world-weary sophisticates like Leslie Howard, Robert Donat, Ronald Colman, and Paul Muni; swashbuckling Errol Flynn, or tall, handsome fellows (like Father) such as Henry Fonda, James Stewart, William Holden, and Gary Cooper.

I will go to thirty-nine picture shows before this year is out, my favorites being *Camille* with Robert Taylor and Greta Garbo; *The Plainsman* with Jean Arthur and Gary Cooper; *Lost Horizon* with Ronald Colman; *The Good Earth* with Paul Muni, and *Seventh Heaven* with James Stewart and Simone Simon.

MAY: ANOTHER TERRIBLE disaster. The giant balloon *Hindenburg* explodes, killing thirty-six. We see this fiery scene over and over on the newsreels every time we go to a picture show.

JUNE: I GRADUATE from Woodlawn. Uvvy and Father give me a pale green Corona portable typewriter in a stout case; I plan to take it on my travels as a foreign correspondent.

Goodbye Miss Stacey Furr after four years in your Latin class.

Goodbye Miss E. Chapman who demonstrates Mohammedanism so memorably by clambering on your desk, kneeling toward the East, rearing your ample rump, and praying to Mecca.

Goodbye Miss Mildred Barnard of the flaming red hair, short temper, and limited tolerance for unfortunates like me with no aptitude for math.

Goodbye Mr. M. P. Gray of the whispery voice. Thank you for selecting me to write for *The Woodlog* and *The Tatler*.

Goodbye Virgil. Sorry about not taking your phone calls. Sorry about giving away those chocolate-covered cherries.


IT IS ALMOST taken for granted that I will go to Birmingham-Southern College; this small Methodist college has high standards, albeit located in a remote corner of the world. Wellesley is not even mentioned, money being still scarce and scholarships—at least to us—unknown. Besides, Father will sleep easier if he knows that I am only one bedroom away.

Although I myself dream of larking around the world like Amelia Earhart and Richard Halliburton, everybody else assumes that, when reality sets in, I will marry and devote myself exclusively to house, husband, and children. So who needs Wellesley—unless to meet a Harvard man!


JULY: AMELIA EARHART, in honor of whom I used to wear that leather aviator cap with goggles and earflaps, disappears into the vast Pacific Ocean without a trace. I'll never forget your freckles and your confident smile, Amelia; surely you'll turn up someday, safe and sound.

Four of the Scottsboro Boys are set free, thanks in part to the stubborn, brave efforts of Dr. Henry M. Edmonds in helping to form the Alabama Scottsboro Fair Trial Committee.

Father, Uvvy, and I drive to Lowndes County deep in Alabama's Black Belt to visit Mary Chappell, the daughter of Father's boss. Mary has just joined the faculty of Calhoun Colored School founded by Northern missionaries after The War Between—oops, the *Civil War*.

VIRGINIA: Met, rode and ate with Negro instructors. Novel.

I have been doing much the same with Audrey, Essie, and Miss Rose's string of retainers my entire life. But I sense a subtle difference. I am eating and riding in automobiles with these teachers almost as if they were *white*!

> VIRGINIA: It was a beautiful night and our regular summer whippoorwill sang his head off. Almost unbearable. I wished for somebody to be with me.

On our summer trip we spend a night at Lexington, Virginia. But I am too old now to be interested in Stonewall Jackson's stuffed horse; I stroll up and down the sidewalk in front of our little inn hoping that one of the boys from Washington and Lee or Virginia Military Institute will speak to me.

At home I no longer swim in little, mud-bottomed Shadow Lake; I lounge away the summer days at the Roebuck Club pool, wearing my new dubonnet and pink Jantzen, sipping what we call a "dope (Coca-Cola) with lime," and whispering to other girls about "the curse."

Like almost everybody else, I gorge on *Gone With the Wind*, reading all night, impatient to learn the fates of Scarlett and Rhett. I even persuade Uvvy to buy me what is billed as a "Gone With the Wind dress" with ruffles, puffed sleeves, and a skirt made entirely of pleats. But above all I am enthralled by Thomas Wolfe, spellbound by his torrents of prose, awash in tears at the end of *Look Homeward Angel*.

AUGUST: FATHER AND I are having serious differences of opinion. He strongly opposes my wearing lipstick and he does not want me to join a sorority.

> VIRGINIA: Had a discussion with Father about lipstick, which he detests but nevertheless I shall use it when I am sixteen. I am going to join a sorority despite Father's objections.

Little coveys of girls from Over the Mountain invite me to meet them downtown at Joy Young's Restaurant where two customers can split a thirty-five-cent Mandarin lunch and have chop suey and noodles to spare.

When I go out into the wide world of Birmingham-Southern College, I will need these girls. They will introduce me to the cutest boys. They will initiate me in the mysterious etiquette of dances at the Pickwick Club: matters like "no breaks," "leadouts," and the "stag line." And they will instruct me to twist my narrow hips and snap my fingers to the rhythm of a new dance craze, The Big Apple.

Clutching the mantelpiece for support in my unprecedented mood of defiance, I give Father what I consider a clincher: I am entitled to my own mistakes!

But Father is unmoved. It is his responsibility, he answers solemnly, to save me from making mistakes in the first place.

Topside: *630 Ridge Road, after it was enlarged in 1937.*

SEPTEMBER: AFTER ALMOST seventeen years of marriage, Dorothy is to have a proper house. *Topside* undergoes a major expansion—columns in front, screen porch moved to the rear, larger dining room, book room for Ted's ever-growing collection, and a new master bedroom. (Their double bed vanishes to make way for the newest fad—*twin* beds.) And at long last, a furnace.

VIRGINIA: Had heat for the first time. It really felt wonderful!

No more dressing on chilly mornings behind the living room stove. Yet I am torn as to whether this is really an improvement. My little bedroom fireplace, with its coal grate glowing dim red in the night, is no more.

VIRGINIA: The Ford salesman sent us out a Lincoln Zephyr to try over the weekend. Grand car.

But Father does not buy the Lincoln Zephyr: too much luxury, he must have figured, is bad for the soul.

I attain the magic age: sixteen. Dorothy presents me with the ring that she

*Dorothy with "Shine" on the back steps of her new house.*

received from her grandmother on her own sixteenth birthday, a few months before she set off for Wellesley. It has five diamonds in a row; I flash them from the ring finger of my right hand. My lips glisten scarlet, pink, tangerine, or mauve, depending on which shade of Coty's lipstick I favor. On the inner sweater of my new twin sweater set, just above the nipple of my modest, left breast, I wear the tiny golden arrow of a Pi Beta Phi pledge.

By quarter to seven every weekday, Uvvy deposits Father and me at the Loop. A big, yellow number thirty-eight streetcar is about to take off for downtown, then on toward the steel mills to the west, passing within five blocks of Birmingham-Southern College. We are regulars; the conductor opens the door to admit the editor, his briefcase bulging with newspapers, and his daughter with her armload of books. He signals to the motorman: Ding-a-ling.

We're off!

∾

PART SIX

*Afterword*

# *What Happened to Everybody?*

DR. ROLAND FRYE, whose private school I attended, taught at the University of Pennsylvania for almost twenty years, served as a research professor at the Folger Shakespeare Library, and wrote eight books on theology and literature. He died in 2005.

EZRA SIMS, my younger schoolmate at The Roland Frye Private School, later studied with Darius Milhaud and became an accomplished composer of microtonal music. He lives in Cambridge, Massachusetts.

VIRGIL THOMSON, my admirer at Woodlawn High School, served as a bombardier in World War II. In January 1944, he died when his plane crashed in England on its return from a raid. Posthumously Lt. Thomson was awarded the Purple Heart.

LEE OLA SHANNON HOLCOMBE, Elizabeth's lifelong friend, married but had no children. In her later years, Lee Ola invited a fortunate niece or nephew to accompany her each year—new ballgowns in her steamer trunk—to Vienna for the opera season at the Stadtsoper.

JOHN MCCLELLAND VAN DER VEER (Daddy Mac) died in 1944 at seventy-eight; he had never been to a doctor. Mac and Rose had been married fifty-two years.

Labrot & Graham, the distillery where Mac worked for thirty years, rising to manager, was bought and restored by Brown-Forman in

HONORED POSTHUMOUSLY— Lt. Virgil Thomson (above), son of Mr. and Mrs. W. E. Thomson of 443 Exeter Drive, Roebuck, has been posthumously awarded the Purple Heart. Lt. Thomson, who had served overseas as bombardier since October, 1943, was killed in the crash landing of his plane on return from a cross-channel raid Jan. 4, 1944. He entered the Army in July, 1941, transferred to the AAF the following year, and received his wings and commission at Childress Field, Tex.

*Rose and Mac—
still a handsome
couple despite
fifty years of hard
times.*

1996. Producing a premier, small-batch bourbon called Woodford Reserve (instead of Old Oscar Pepper), the site is a major tourist attraction in the Bluegrass region of Kentucky.

ROSE STEWART VAN DER VEER (Miss Rose), who so determinedly resisted growing old, became senile. Her family came to the reluctant conclusion that they could no longer care for her themselves. Probably she was not conscious of her destination but, as she was being carried up the steps of what we then called an old-age home, Miss Rose resisted one last time—she died at the door.

Rose and Mac are buried in the beautiful, old cemetery overlooking Frankfort, Kentucky, near their relatives, the friends of their youth, and next to a small stone marking the grave of their baby, Eleanor.

Rose's marker bears this inscription:

ROSE STEWART
WIFE OF J. M. VAN DER VEER
DIED SEPTEMBER 2, 1955

Not only is she buried under the name she bore during her glory days but—even more important to Miss Rose—no Frankfort busybody would ever discover her most carefully guarded secret: the date of her birth. (Ssh—she was eighty-nine.)

MCCLELLAN VAN DER VEER (Teddy, Ted) became editor of the *Birmingham News*. In 1942, he was elected a Nieman Fellow at Harvard University. He won several awards from the Freedoms Foundation of Valley Forge, Pennsylvania. During the second World War, he broadcast a weekly commentary over radio station WSGN. Because he could not see his audience, his voice came across steady and strong.

In 1959, Ted voluntarily informed his employers that he was to reach the customary retirement age of sixty-five the following year. No formal records existing at that time, they had believed him to be much younger. He was retired January 1, 1960.

Retirement brought on Ted's second nervous collapse. He underwent a series of shock treatments; as a result, he returned to a semblance of normality.

The following year, he and Dorothy made their first trip to Europe, a driving tour that, as always, they themselves planned. They sailed home on the *Liberté*; on the night of their arrival Ted died of a massive stroke in New York, the city from which mental illness had driven him forty years before. To Dorothy at his side, he whispered his last words:

*I am so afraid.*

Posthumously, Ted Van der Veer was elected to the Alabama Newspaper Hall of Fame at Auburn University. Years later, when I gave talks around Alabama, elderly men and women made a point of coming up to tell me that they had admired my father's editorials; one showed me a yellowed editorial that she had saved for years. Nobody writes like that anymore, they told me.

After Ted's death, Rose Graves, wife of John Temple Graves II, sent our family one of his editorials that she had treasured because it spoke of her mother, Mrs. Ross Smith, whose family owned Wilson Chapel. The date is unknown but obviously the era is that of World War II.

*Ted at home with his books.*

Editorial: "When The Jonquils Bloom"

A lady says, "Come to see us when the jonquils bloom." She did not say "if the jonquils bloom," she said "when the jonquils bloom."

Maybe we will get by there, kind lady, but even more than the invitation we appreciate the way you said it, "when the jonquils bloom." In the calm acceptance of the fact that the jonquils will bloom again, there was all the faith that the beauty of the world will persist, all the wisdom and experience which knows that wars and rumors of war cannot stop the return of spring.

The lady spoke in midwinter. But soon the Spring will come back to

Jones Valley. Soon her yard, and let us be glad, many other yards in and around Birmingham will be bright with the yellow that seems too brilliant to have been caught from March's pale sun and must have been carried over from last summer.

No matter what happens to Hitler, the jonquils will be back. No matter how the tides of hatred spread over the world, the jonquils will bloom again . . . No matter what of life or death may be our fate, the jonquils will be here soon.

And so we thank you, gracious lady, partly for the invitation, but much more for the reminder that the jonquils will bloom again, and again, and again.

(Courtesy of the *Birmingham News*)

Writing editorials (usually lead editorials) seven days a week from 1935 until his retirement in 1959, (except during his annual two-week vacations), Ted's output was voluminous. All may be found either in the *Birmingham Age-Herald* or, after 1943, in the *Birmingham News*. A few of his editorials, several portraits, two of his unpublished manuscripts, his obituary, and some personal letters regarding him are housed in the Department of Archives and Manuscripts, Birmingham Public Library.

My father's unpublished, 461-page autobiographical novel, "Though He Falters," describing his nervous breakdown, is on deposit in the Archives of the Historical Collections Department, Lister Hill Library of the Health Sciences, the University of Alabama at Birmingham. It is available for research by medical professionals in or entering the study of mental illness.

In a lengthy editorial on the death of McClellan "Ted" Van der Veer, E. L. Holland, Jr., his successor, wrote, in part:

He [Ted] literally grappled with philosophy. In kinship with truly intellectual pursuit, he sought the matter of man and his religious needs. Ted Van der Veer was ever the entirely civilized man; his search was to find forms of order. These make it possible for man to live with man, for society to emerge, improve.

(Courtesy of the *Birmingham News*)

STEWART VAN DER VEER wrote three novels, all quickly forgotten. He retired early, bought a farm, and constructed fish ponds. He wrote an autobiographical novel that was never published. Ironically, it was the pulps that gave him a measure of fame. Many years after Stewart died in 1966 at seventy-three, I received a letter from a history doctoral candidate at a Midwestern university who was at work on a dissertation about pulp magazines and those who wrote for them. He sought information about Stewart Van der Veer, whose frequent by-line he had noted. Stewart's letters from the Italian front during the first World War, deposited in the Birmingham Public Library Archives, have been consulted many times by students of that war.

DOROTHY RAINOLD VAN DER VEER, after she became a widow, traveled to Switzerland, the British Isles, Scandinavia, the Soviet Union, Japan, Hong Kong, and India. However her happiest trip was to Wellesley College in 1969 for the first time since her graduation fifty years before. She died at a retirement community in 1984 at eighty-six. Actually, for Dorothy, life had lost its purpose after Ted's death.

ELIZABETH VAN DER VEER spent her final years in a retirement community; for the first time in her life, she felt safe and secure. She took great pleasure in writing this community's newsletter, *Chirps*. Halley's Comet came around a second time during her lifetime; like most of us, she heard about it but could not see it. She died in 1993 at ninety-one. Her obituary described her as one of Birmingham's pioneer women in advertising, mentioned her short stories, and noted that she had been a member of Kappa Kappa Gamma.

Readers interested in the pulp magazines of the 1930s will find eight of her "love stories" and some miscellany in the Elizabeth Van der Veer Papers, Department of Archives and Manuscripts, Birmingham Public Library.

UNLIKE THE WANDERING Van der Veers, I have remained in place except for a few years during the second World War. However, I no longer live in Roebuck Springs. That once-rural bohemia is now a typical, middle-class suburb; I might not recognize my old neighborhood except for Wilson Chapel and a couple of little, spring-fed lakes. Its residents speed downtown via Interstate-20; those lumbering yellow streetcars, so vital to our lives, have long been retired.

Since I arrived here as a child, Birmingham has undergone a major trans-formation: its steel and cotton mills closed (Sloss Furnace, cold and lifeless, a museum of the pig iron industry; Avondale Mill and its village demolished), its major employer now The University of Alabama at Birmingham, a nationally ranked medical facility.

But to call Birmingham The Magic City—the booster slogan that lured so many, including my grandfather—is no longer fitting. Birmingham's name evokes, not magical growth, but images of Bull Connor's fire hoses and police dogs and of the tragic bombing of the Sixteenth Street Baptist Church. On a more positive note, legal segregation has vanished and blacks have shed their age-old posture of servility. For middle-class blacks, opportunities are virtually unlimited. Were they living today, Audrey, with her warm personality, could well be a television anchor; Essie, with his outsized stature, might even be the mayor. But Mac was right about one thing: the climate of Birmingham is close to ideal, thanks to nature—and air conditioning.

Initially, I took up Father's profession, becoming one of the early women reporters for the *Birmingham News* and, during the second World War, for the Washington bureau of the Associated Press.

I left journalism for academe, earned a Ph.D., chaired a history department, and taught college students for twenty-five years. I wrote eight books of history (see page ii).

Like Miss Rose and Dorothy, I married for love and beauty, having met a handsome man by pure chance. My marriage, like that of my grandparents and parents, endured through hard times and heart-breaking events.

The Great Depression left its mark on me, as it did on millions of Americans of my generation. Almost seventy years later, we still eat leftovers, save clothes and shoes long out of style, switch off the lights when we leave a room, reuse aluminum foil and Christmas wrappings, even spread paper towels out to dry. But I no longer eat burnt toast.

Those summer trips also had a lasting effect; I am an inveterate traveler. I prefer to plan my own itinerary and I am always on time—figuratively speak-ing, sitting on my suitcase. If there is no prospect of a trip during the brutal heat of summer, I bring out the white slipcovers and—praise be to its little known inventor—I turn on the air conditioning.

I have a lesser tendency than did my elders toward High Romanticism. I have never visualized myself in a role, as did Miss Rose the Belle and Stewart the Cowboy. I do not try to hide my age. But I do color my hair and often, in the middle of winter, I look in the mirror and am amused at the sight of my reflection clad in white.

I am not a joiner of clubs but my reasons are not as lofty as were my father's. Like Father, I have many unanswered questions on the subject of religion yet I maintain my lifelong membership in the Independent Presbyterian Church. I make no pretense of matching Father's purity of thought and deed. If I arrive at my overdue parking space and find no ticket on the windshield, I jump in my car, leaving the meter unpaid. As I hasten away, I can almost hear a familiar refrain:

*No one can corrupt me but myself!*

# *Reflections on Anxiety*

I had a happy childhood. I hope that came across in this memoir. Looking back from the brink of my eighty-eighth year, I realize what a rich experience my family gave me despite the fact that we lived perilously close to the poverty line. The things I learned to treasure as a child—books, nature, sports, food, music, travel—have been the joys of my life.

I grew up with no awareness that I lived in the midst of a family crippled by fear. I accepted my grandfather's silence as normal behavior. I took it for granted that Miss Rose would be pacing the porch if I were two minutes late arriving at her home. I thought nothing about the fact that my aunt and uncle, in their thirties and forties (and always), still lived with their parents. I had no knowledge of my father's nervous collapse.

In the course of writing this memoir, I came across a great deal of evidence as to the presence of anxiety in my small family circle. I learned for the first time that my grandfather, Daddy Mac, as a young husband and father, had suffered from what was then called "nervous prostration." I noted how many times Elizabeth, in her diary, referred to Mac's silent moods and withdrawal from everyday life. It occurred to me that Mac—not Rose—may have been a genetic carrier of depression.

But anxiety also overwhelmed Miss Rose after the death of her baby, Eleanor. She began to fear other deaths in her family; she forced Mac to sell their house in New Orleans and move his family to a boardinghouse so she could spend her entire time worrying whether her sons would be killed in the first World War. That particular fear led her to become an ardent advocate of the League of Nations and, later, of American isolationism. In her unending religious quest, Miss Rose sought to convince herself of reincarnation or, preferably, life after death.

Elizabeth feared the uncertainty of married life, especially parenthood. She quickly recoiled from marriage, retreating to the comparative safety of living at home with her mother, father, and brother.

Stewart, in his autobiographical novel, described his own experience with fear when he served in the U.S. Army during the Great War. But Stewart romanticized this episode, as he did almost everything in his life. To keep his fears at bay, Stewart assumed various roles: opera singer, outdoorsman, possum hunter, novelist. He, too, shrank from taking on the responsibilities of husband and father. In mid-life—after the time period covered in this memoir— Stewart was briefly married to a much younger woman. Even then, Stewart and his wife lived, literally and figuratively, under Miss Rose's roof.

Teddy, the most gifted and promising of Rose and Mac's children, was also the most vulnerable. As a small boy, he feared speaking in public; thus he was never able to become a minister or a college professor. He could, however, preach and teach in his anonymous editorials. And he could talk to people over the radio.

All these fears afflicted my elders long before mood-altering drugs became available. Just rest, a doctor told Ted, chop wood, hoe weeds. Mac never consulted a doctor in his entire lifetime; Elizabeth stayed in bed on weekends, trying to recover on her own from some mysterious illness because she could not afford to pay a doctor. With no help from medicine or psychiatry, my family soldiered on. Simple pleasures sustained us—singing, reading, playing softball. And above all, humor proved to be our saving grace.

As an adult, I witnessed Father's second breakdown, the result of his abrupt loss of his life's work as an editorial writer. I thought that shock treatments had restored him to normality. I last saw my father striding through a dark piazza in Rome, holding my mother's hand. He seemed like his old self, relishing a trip. But when those European travels came to an end, fear overwhelmed him again and, I believe, brought about his sudden death at sixty-six.

After I entered middle age, anxiety gradually, stealthily afflicted me. I had believed myself impervious to this family disability, thanks, perhaps, to my fearless mother. But I began to experience irrational imaginings of personal and family catastrophes; like Miss Rose, I visualize car accidents by the thousands, sudden illnesses, and other commonplace fears. Unlike my father, I have never been so overwhelmed that I have been unable to function in the workplace; indeed, I have kept my anxiety pretty well concealed and I seem, to all outward appearances, untroubled. But fears wake me in the night and I cry out:

*No! No! No!*

*Rock Mountain, viewed from High Hampton Inn.*

# Acknowledgments

I express my appreciation to the late Bill McKee and to his son, Will McKee, for providing me with food, shelter, and quiet for a month at their beautiful High Hampton Inn and Country Club, Cashiers, North Carolina, while I gathered my thoughts and arranged my notes for this book.

I thank *The Register* of the Kentucky Historical Society, the University of Alabama Press, and the New York *Times* for permission to use excerpts from my previously published writings. I thank the Herbert Hoover Library, West Branch, Iowa, for copies of Rose Van der Veer's letters.

I thank the *Birmingham News* for permission to reprint one of McClellan (Ted) Van der Veer's editorials.

I thank many contemporaries who helped me to recall details of our lives during the Great Depression.